HOW TO PROFIT FROM THE COMING OIL CRISIS

HOW TO PROFIT FROM THE COMING OIL CRISIS

KURT WULFF
WITH
BILL BRUNS

A JOHN BOSWELL BOOK

BANTAM BOOKS
TORONTO • NEW YORK • LONDON • SYDNEY • AUCKLAND

HOW TO PROFIT FROM THE COMING OIL CRISIS
A Bantam Book / March 1988

Library of Congress Cataloging-in-Publication Data

Wulff, Kurt.
How to profit from the coming oil crisis.

"A John Boswell book."
Includes index.
1. Petroleum industry and trade.   2. Commodity
exchanges.   3. Investments.   I. Bruns, Bill.   II. Title.
HG6047.P47W84   1988   332.63'22   87-47901
ISBN 0-553-05287-X

Published simultaneously in the United States and Canada

Bantam Books are published by Bantam Books, a division
of Bantam Doubleday Dell Publishing Group, Inc. Its trade-
mark, consisting of the words "Bantam Books" and the por-
trayal of a rooster, is Registered in U.S. Patent and Trademark
Office and in other countries. Marca Registrada. Bantam
Books, 666 Fifth Avenue, New York, New York 10103.

PRINTED IN THE UNITED STATES OF AMERICA
DH   0 9 8 7 6 5 4 3 2 1

Dedicated to my wife, Louise,
and to the memory of my parents.

ACKNOWLEDGMENTS

Many persons helped me achieve a rewarding investment career and helped translate the lessons learned into book form.

First I thank my clients who thought that my work deserved compensation to Donaldson, Lufkin & Jenrette and to me.

At DLJ I thank the persons in sales, trading, research, and support operations who marketed my ideas, sought commissions, critiqued, and published my findings. John Chalsty backed me from the day he hired me through the day he became chief executive officer. Helen Potter, my assistant for more than ten years, greatly enhanced my productivity with her organization and communication skills combined with loyal dedication and friendship.

There could not have been research without industry sources. Corporate chiefs, financial executives, operating officers, and workers in the field have nearly always been helpful when asked, and many volunteered assistance.

For learning about the industry before working on Wall Street I am indebted to my colleagues while at Arthur D. Little and Chevron. I thank Harvard Business School and my mother-in-law who loaned me the tuition for Harvard and forgave the loan when I received my degree. The late Professor Roland Ragatz at the University of Wisconsin helped me with scholarships, assistantships, and valuable recommendations. Many more friends and family have encouraged me along the way.

The press has treated me well for which I am grateful, especially to those who featured me prominently. Thanks to the public relations group at DLJ for introducing me to Gad Romann who introduced me to John Boswell who in turn brought me together with Bill Bruns and Bantam Books.

Without question, Bill Bruns worked hardest on this book. Starting with my published research going back to 1971, Bill extracted the best material and repackaged it in compact, readable form. Attending my presentations and reading my new pieces as though he was my most active client for the past two years, Bill was always enthusiastic while trying to fit new information into an investment framework. Finally we both thank Peter Guzzardi, our editor at Bantam, for his unflagging support.

—Kurt Wulff
Short Hills, New Jersey
October 20, 1987

CONTENTS

HOW TO
PROFIT FROM
THE COMING
OIL CRISIS

CHAPTER 1

LOOKING UP
FROM THE BOTTOM
OF THE WELL

*H*ow easily we forget the trauma of a national energy crisis.

The year was 1979 and Americans were reeling from the second energy shock of the decade. It was a time of panic buying at gasoline stations; fistfights at the gas pumps; canceled vacation plans; a national 55 mph speed limit; bleak visions of an energy-restricted future; and President Carter's dramatic television address, in which he vowed, "Never again will our nation's independence be hostage to foreign oil."

The president had proposed a program to help secure energy self-sufficiency for the country, but as the crisis eased—resolved not by governmental actions but by inexorable supply and demand factors—so did the opportunity to implement urgent, lasting safeguards. Now, nearly a decade later, the United States is still confronted by a pervasive, long-term danger: its ultimate dependence on

Middle East oil. And once again the stage is set for another devastating energy crunch that could indeed dwarf what happened to the world in 1973 and 1979, when warfare and revolution in the Persian Gulf region brought about supply cutbacks and sharply escalating oil prices.

This is not only my conviction as an oil and gas analyst on Wall Street, but the opinion of various executives in the energy business. For example:

- L. W. Funkhouser, a vice-president of Chevron, now retired: "We are setting ourselves up for a real oil crisis —one that will make those of the 1970s look mild."
- Thomas Cruikshank, chief executive of Halliburton, an oil services company: "It's going to come as a shock when the oil crisis replays itself, but it's going to happen."
- Fred Hartley, chairman of Unocal: "The decline in U.S. production and the rise in oil imports—if unchecked—will soon reach alarming proportions. By 1990 or before, America could depend on foreign sources for more than half of its petroleum supplies— the highest level in our history. Without decisive action in Washington, this nation will once again become a hostage to OPEC's plans and policies."

OIL: A FINITE RESOURCE AT RISK

Why is the United States in this predicament once again, how inevitable is "Oil Shock III," and—this time around— what does it all mean to you as a stock market investor?

2

Let's start with two fundamental facts about oil.

First, *oil will remain an indispensable and irreplaceable commodity over the foreseeable future.* While emphasizing the potential of coal, nuclear, and other alternative energy resources, Energy Secretary John Herrington has stressed the fact that "our economic and energy security is inextricably tied to the fate and fortunes of our domestic petroleum industry through this century." Adds Amoco chairman Richard Morrow: "There is no substitute on the horizon for petroleum transportation fuels—to run our automobiles, trucks, trains, and airplanes." Synthetic fuels such as shale oil and methanol could eventually become viable alternatives, but only when oil prices are well above $30 a barrel and the country's energy well-being is under siege.

Second, *oil is a nonrenewable energy source and we're burning our known supplies much faster than we're finding new reserves, particularly in the United States, but also practically anywhere outside the Middle East.* The industrial world is not suddenly going to run out of oil, but the trends—distinct and ominous—will make the United States increasingly vulnerable to international developments as the Persian Gulf countries strengthen their grip on the world oil market.

A PERILOUS DECLINE IN U.S. OIL PRODUCTION

America's growing reliance on imported oil (once again past 40 percent) stems from the fact that crude oil production began a decline in 1986 that may prove irreversible.

Total daily U.S. *output* peaked at about 10.5 million barrels per day in 1985, will average about 9.9 million in 1987, and could slump to 9.2 million in 1988. Meanwhile, total U.S. oil *demand* has been rising modestly in recent years to about 16.5 million barrels per day—without the stimulus of a robust economy and despite conservation measures implemented in the late 1970s that are now built into the country's infrastructure and economy.

The result is a shortfall of about 6 million barrels per day between U.S. production and consumer demand. Given the trends already in place, this gap will continue expanding and will dictate a significantly higher percentage of oil imports. After all, demand is unlikely to slacken and it's unrealistic to hope that U.S. producers can reverse the country's declining production trend.

One reason for this pessimism is the fact that U.S. oil output will continue to reflect the disastrous impact of sharply lower oil prices in 1986. As prices plunged that year toward $10 per barrel, U.S. companies slashed exploration and drilling budgets by billions of dollars while shutting down thousands of uneconomic wells that may never flow again.

These severe cutbacks continued into 1987, further depressing U.S. output over the near term while heightening concerns about where our new oil will come from in 1990 and beyond to replace current reserves. As one oilman reminds us, "Tomorrow's oil is found with today's investment." But not until oil prices reach about $25 and appear headed for $30—thus offering the necessary economic incentive—will we be seeing aggressive exploration and drilling programs once again. Even then, it can take eight to ten years after a major discovery is made before oil is actually flowing to market. This obviously postpones any "quick fixes" for U.S. production much before 1995.

4

A more fundamental concern is raised by the bleak prospects for meaningful oil exploration in the United States, even with much higher oil prices.

Like a giant pincushion, the onshore areas of the lower forty-eight states have been 98 percent explored and the easy oil has been pumped or already discovered; what's left is increasingly harder to find or uneconomical to produce at today's prices. Even Exxon officials, who can tap the deepest coffers in the business, admit they are reluctant to spend heavily on oil exploration in the United States because of geological limitations. We know, for example, that the biggest field in an oil basin is usually found first, and succeeding discoveries in that basin are smaller and at deeper—and thus more expensive—levels. "It's like having an Easter egg hunt with ostrich eggs and hummingbird eggs," said one oilman. "You're going to find the ostrich eggs first."

Exploring new basins is therefore the obvious strategy for finding large new oil fields. Unfortunately, most of the known basins in the United States have been well explored, except for about six or eight offshore basins in Alaska and the Bering Sea, plus prospective areas offshore of California and in deep-water sections of the Gulf of Mexico. Expensive drilling in the Alaska basins has proven unsuccessful thus far, and environmental opposition may prevent meaningful exploration and subsequent drilling in new areas off the California coast. Meanwhile, promising Gulf projects require the prospect and support of much higher crude oil prices.

Oil companies also need considerable luck when pursuing "hostile environment" exploration projects, since the investment of billions of dollars to explore promising areas is no guarantee (1) that oil will actually be discovered or (2) that it will be economically feasible to produce.

As just one example, Exxon, Mobil, and others sought a blockbuster discovery offshore in the Atlantic—the infamous Baltimore Canyon play—and it proved a billion-dollar bust. Mukluk, in offshore Alaska, represents a more recent billion-dollar dry hole. Little wonder that enthusiastic spending for exploration in the United States has declined in recent years, not only due to depressed oil prices but because results have not justified all the efforts and investment.

As a result, warns Interior Secretary Donald Hodel, "There is a continuing deterioration of our ability to produce oil in the United States. Down the road we simply won't have wells to replace the ones that are producing now."

Lacking any apparent billion-barrel frontier discoveries that could have a meaningful impact on U.S. production, the domestic industry must resort to finding smaller and smaller fields within the existing known basins. On that basis, we certainly can't expect to replace current production with new reserves in the coming years, especially as Alaskan output—now about 20 percent of U.S. production—goes into normal decline starting in 1988. Couple this accelerating decline with just a modest increase in yearly consumption and the United States will be importing over 50 percent of its oil by 1990, if not earlier, leaving the country increasingly vulnerable to supply disruptions and price manipulations. Remember, the original oil crisis in 1973 occurred when the United States had only a 33 percent dependency on foreign oil.

LITTLE 'RESCUE' POTENTIAL BY NON-OPEC PRODUCERS

I'm often asked why there's such concern about our growing reliance on imported oil, other than the substantial impact it has on our foreign trade deficit. After all, since the United States has only about 5 percent of the world's known reserves, why not conserve this relatively meager supply by drawing on willing exporters with ample reserves, especially those in the Middle East?

The implication, of course, is that if an energy crisis is indeed triggered by the actions of Persian Gulf producers, or events in that part of the world, the United States can calmly and logically respond in two ways: first, by drawing on existing inventories and oil stored in the Strategic Petroleum Reserve, a series of hollow salt domes on the Gulf Coast; and second, by simply importing more oil from Western suppliers such as Canada, Mexico, and Great Britain (and perhaps even a "friendly" OPEC producer like Venezuela, forgetting that it has always aligned itself with official OPEC policy).

Alas, that kind of strategic thinking simply won't work in this imperfect world.

The main argument against consuming all of the cheap foreign supply available and not developing domestic supply is that when we need the oil in a crisis, we won't have it. Yes, the reserves will be there, but not the necessary production and delivery systems. Inevitably, there is a lag time between the decision to develop new capacity when an actual crisis occurs and the time when that capacity becomes available. The lag time amounts to months, even years if we're talking about drilling new wells and building

pipelines and other facilities to deliver this oil to its necessary markets.

The second crucial argument against complacency is
that non-OPEC producers, as a group, will be hard-pressed
to increase their current production levels by 1990, let
alone meet growing worldwide demand. As a result, incre-
mental increases in oil demand by Western countries—
beyond today's levels—will have to be met by OPEC
producers, thus giving them greater ability to manipulate
the world's oil market.

Some observers are cheered by the encouraging prospects for oil production in many parts of the world, noting
that countries like Norway, Brazil, Colombia, India, Ma-
laysia, Vietnam, Angola, Oman, and North Yemen are
developing important new fields. Yet while this resulting
new output could add over 1 million barrels per day to the
world's supply by 1990, it will basically only cover anticipated production declines in the United States, Canada,
and maturing North Sea fields.

What about increased production by the Soviet Union
and China to lessen world dependence on OPEC oil? These
countries have long been viewed as a potential trump card
on OPEC domination with their seemingly vast untapped
potential, but neither is likely to play that key role this
century. Although the Soviet Union should remain the
world's largest oil producer, its actual exports to the Western world should show little increase into the early 1990s.
Any additional Chinese output will easily be soaked up by
increased domestic demand as the country becomes more
industrialized.

Ultimately, as we extend these worldwide developments into 1990, OPEC producers stand to gain decisive
control of the oil market, even if only through inescapable
economic trends. Current non-OPEC production is near

capacity, and without significant new discoveries coming on stream to provide greater potential capacity, supply will remain too inelastic to satisfy even a modest increase in yearly demand. Over time, of course, more wells can be drilled and pipelines built to deliver more oil on a daily basis from non-OPEC supply, but only with the incentive of higher prices.

Thus, given these circumstances, any subsequent increased demand for OPEC oil will (1) help diminish a worldwide oversupply of oil, thereby easing any downward pressure on oil prices, and (2) allow OPEC producers to gain a greater market share. With a larger pie to share, they can increase their production limits while maintaining a stable oil price that can be maneuvered higher more easily and with greater conviction in the years ahead.

A DECISIVE ROLE FOR PERSIAN GULF PRODUCERS

A disturbing consequence of these developments is that power within OPEC will shift increasingly to the volatile Persian Gulf states—Saudi Arabia, Iran, Iraq, Kuwait, and United Arab Emirates in particular—for they are the only cartel members with sufficient export capacity to meet continually growing worldwide demand.

One study, for example, estimates that by the 1990s, five of OPEC's thirteen members—Ecuador, Gabon, Nigeria, Indonesia, and Algeria—will need all the oil they produce for their own consumption. This means that OPEC exports would have to be largely met by the other eight members, six of whom are in the Persian Gulf region (the sixth member being Qatar, a minor producer).

That oil's future may hinge chiefly on developments in the Middle East has perhaps been the world's fate since the resource was created millions of years ago. Although it was distributed widely around the globe, an inordinate supply was left for eventual Middle East countries. To appreciate the scope of Mother Nature's legacy, remember that a "major" oil field is defined as one having recoverable reserves of 100 million barrels; a "giant" is 1 billion barrels and "super giants" contain 5 billion. Out of some thirty thousand oil fields discovered around the world this century, thirty-seven have been classified as super giants. They contain about 35 percent of all the oil ever discovered. Of these thirty-seven super giants, only eleven lie outside the Middle East, and just two have been discovered in the past twenty years outside the Middle East— Cantarell in Mexico and Alaska's North Slope. Chances are slim that another super giant field will soon be discovered in non-OPEC frontiers.

Not only do the OPEC members in the Middle East hold an estimated 57 percent of the Free World's proven oil reserves, they control the world's most prolific and low-cost fields. This means that as major fields in the United States and elsewhere around the world are played out and require higher-cost production—leaving non-OPEC countries hard-pressed to increase production—the Middle East producers will become the ultimate supplier of oil to most energy-dependent nations. More specifically, the Persian Gulf exporters, who sit atop enormous reserves, will have an ever-increasing ability to dictate production and pricing on the world market.

So as we look out to the near horizon, our guard lowered by the far-reaching consequences of recent developments, Oil Shock III is staring us down. "We are heading toward a period of time when we will be sitting in gas lines," warned Interior Secretary Donald Hodel in February 1987. His estimated time frame: "Any time in the next two to five years."

World geology and the unyielding forces of economic supply and demand alone could bring about this next energy crunch as the industrial world grows increasingly dependent on OPEC oil. But this scenario doesn't even factor in the explosive influence of events in the Persian Gulf region that can leave the United States dangerously vulnerable to oil shortages and price increases for years to come. A crisis could be ignited at any time by any number of incidents capable of causing supply disruptions. For example:

- A supply cutoff could be orchestrated by certain OPEC members who try to use oil as a weapon to influence U.S. foreign policy, as we saw happen with the 1973 Arab oil embargo.
- A revolution could take millions of barrels of oil off the market, similar to the aftermath of the Iranian revolution in early 1979.
- Continuing tensions in the Middle East could lead to a new regional war.
- The Iran-Iraq war could spread to the area's key oil producers: Saudi Arabia, Kuwait, and the United Arab Emirates.
- Military activity in the Persian Gulf waters could block the region's normal flow of oil.
- Pipeline sabotage is always a possibility.

Actually, our *short-term* vulnerability to disruptions in oil supply from the Middle East is more psychological than real, given the millions of barrels of oil in tankers around the world at any particular time. Moreover, our Strategic Petroleum Reserve now contains over 500 million barrels and can be drawn down at a rate of up to 2.1 million barrels a day—or about a third of our daily imports for eight months.

However, history, human nature, and logic tell us that any developments that force the United States to actually *use* the Strategic Petroleum Reserve would trigger consumer hysteria and send oil prices skyrocketing, similar to what happened in the 1970s. "It doesn't take much of a surplus to make a glut," said one oilman, "and it takes even less of a shortage to create a panic." A supply shortfall of only 5 percent in 1979 brought nightmarish gasoline lines and other forms of rationing.

The psychological impact of a major disruption of oil supplies into the United States is a frightening enough prospect. A more disturbing situation, when compared to the 1979 oil crisis, is the absence of foreseeable options to easily overcome sustained oil shortages and soaring fuel costs. While existing inventories would cushion any short-term interruptions in supply, disaster looms beyond a six- to eight-month time frame. Very simply, the United States doesn't have a Prudhoe Bay coming on stream as we did in the 1970s, nor can the non-OPEC world look to a Mexico or a North Sea as major new oil sources to help offset the reliance on OPEC imports.

Realistically, until events force oil prices dramatically higher and encourage greater exploration and production efforts, there's little the U.S. oil industry can do to fore-stall the next energy crisis—and even less the government seems willing to do. History tells us that only a major new calamity will inspire greater conservation efforts ("The moral equivalent of war," declared President Carter) and bring about crash programs to increase oil production and develop a viable synfuels industry (e.g., methanol and shale oil production) and alternate energy sources such as solar, wind, and thermal.

Yet even with massive spending efforts in a time of crisis, we still couldn't expect to reverse declining U.S. oil production overnight in response to a persistent shortage of foreign supply. Noting that the domestic energy industry had been "seriously wounded" by the plunge in oil prices in 1986, George Mitchell, president of Mitchell Energy in Texas, commented that "even if there were immediate large increases in oil prices, it's not conceivable that America's oil production capacity could return to mid-1985 levels in less than four years."

HOW TO PROFIT AS THE ENERGY SQUEEZE WORSENS

Clearly, a new oil shock is heading our way as the converging forces discussed in this chapter impact on the world. I have never considered myself a doomsayer, but I am a realist who knows that the United States must one day pay the consequences for what is happening today in the energy business. Even if the country somehow escapes a traumatic crisis, we have a weakening capacity to respond effectively when conditions create energy shortages and sharply higher energy prices.

I'm also a realist in the sense that if we're going to be victimized by an energy crunch, we can at least profit as investors. Instead of wasting our anger and frustration in

13

outrage against U.S. oil and gas companies and their inevitable runaway profits, why not own stock in some of these select companies and reap gains for your own investment portfolio? Just as in the 1970s, stock market investors will harvest their own "windfall" profits when conditions once again send oil prices through the roof and propel energy stocks to record levels.

Yet the beauty of the investment approach I will be stressing in this book is that you need not be a "doom and gloom" type of investor to take advantage of this exceptional opportunity to buy into the oil patch in the months ahead. You are hedging against the next energy crisis, but you won't need an actual disaster in order to make a lot of money by owning the stocks I recommend.

Here's my strategy, building upon the thesis I have developed to this point.

First, as we *anticipate* a new boom era in the oil and gas industry, you should position yourself in what I consider the most promising long-term stocks.

Second, you should invest in key undervalued stocks, notably from the integrated oil group, that could provide more immediate payoffs through restructuring and takeovers. These selected stocks will also be carried higher by improving industry trends.

My specific advice in this book reflects the fact that my livelihood as an analyst depends on how well I can identify a future trend early and then spotlight the stocks that can best profit from that trend within a reasonable period of time. I can afford to be patient with my own portfolio of stocks as I wait for my ideas to pay off, but many of my institutional clients are under pressure to show performance results the next quarter or two, and they need to have stocks with a more short-term payoff potential.

Thus, I've devised an analytical technique—tested

and refined by my seventeen years experience on Wall Street—that will help you identify energy stocks with significant appreciation potential, whether oil prices simply trend slowly upward in the years ahead or suddenly explode to the upside. My "McDep" technique, utilizing a valuation ratio that spotlights undervalued companies, will show you how to focus on the most likely winners from among the one hundred companies that I cover in my ongoing research.

Here briefly are my three major investment themes, aimed at positioning a part of your investment portfolio in a balance of energy stocks. Of course, nobody can guarantee future developments, but even if you doubt that oil prices can again reach their historic highs by 1990, you should still think hard about investing in this area, thereby protecting your portfolio. You should be able to make money on oil and gas fundamentals alone.

THEME NUMBER ONE:
BUY U.S. OIL AND GAS RESERVES IN THE STOCK MARKET

When you begin building an "energy fund" within your overall investment portfolio (as I'll discuss in detail in Chapter 7), emphasize companies that have a concentrated ownership of high-quality oil and natural gas reserves, particularly in the United States. This will place you in stocks that should thrive for years to come as the United States becomes increasingly dependent on insecure foreign oil and investors place greater value on companies with secure domestic reserves.

Higher oil prices alone will create greater value for current production and reserves in the ground, thus strength-

15

ening a company's ongoing financial performance and underlying value. Now imagine the explosive impact on stock prices if key foreign supplies are suddenly unavailable and investors frantically bid for those companies that have significant reserves safely inside the United States or in secure regions such as the North Sea or Canada.

Basically, your concern should be the strategic value of oil and gas resources as irreplaceable commodities in a rising price environment. This search emphasizes companies with more than 50 percent of their property value in oil and gas reserves, which in turn means greater commodity leverage for your stock as energy prices continue to rise. A high percentage of reserves gives you a purer play, as opposed to owning similar reserves in a company that has most of its property value represented by businesses that are nonsensitive or inversely sensitive to rising oil and gas prices (e.g., refineries, chemicals, and minerals).

The second element of commodity leverage is the company's potential production output, suggested and highlighted by what we know as the "reserve-life index." I calculate this index by taking a company's reported reserves and dividing by the previous year's production. My emphasis is then on long-life reserves, which have a longer projected production life than the industry average and are depleted at a slower rate over time than short-life reserves.

Long-life reserves not only offer the investor greater short-term protection if oil and gas prices fail to rise as quickly as anticipated, but ultimately yield a greater long-term payoff for your original investment. By buying long-life reserves in the stock market at today's prices, you acquire future oil and gas production that can come on stream when energy prices are considerably higher. In a sense, the short-reserve-life companies are going to create greater opportunities for the long-reserve-life companies. As the production capacity for these short-life companies falls, the worth of the remaining resources at long-life companies will increase. I will be guiding you toward the companies with long-life reserves throughout the book.

This fundamental emphasis on oil and gas reserves reflects my conviction that the value of these reserves in the ground bottomed in 1986, is now on an uptrend, and could reach its former peak in the next few years—perhaps by 1990. In fact, you should be buying my recommended stocks with the anticipation that oil prices could equal their historic 1981 highs. At that peak, oil was valued at $12 a barrel in the ground and had an official "contract" price of $35 on the world market. By comparison, oil in mid-1987 was worth $8 in the ground and about $20 on the spot market.

This means that the value of oil and gas in the ground could appreciate by about 50 percent in the next few years if oil prices approach their former highs. And that in turn represents a *100 percent* appreciation potential for several of my favorite stocks, thanks to financial and operating leverage at these companies as underlying property values track oil prices ever higher.

Under this scenario, for example, Texaco would move from $32 to $93 by 1990 (or whenever oil in the ground is again valued at $12 a barrel), Unocal from $29 to $102, Kerr-McGee from $36 to $75, Amoco from $60 to $162, and Dorchester Hugoton—my choicest natural gas play—would climb from $14 to $41.

THEME NUMBER TWO:
SEEK OUT 'PURE PLAYS' IN NATURAL GAS

Capitalize on the coming recovery—and a sustained boom—in natural gas prices by investing in one or more of the "pure play" producers in the prolific Hugoton field of Kansas and Oklahoma. The prime candidates are Dorchester Hugoton, Plains Petroleum, Mesa Limited Partnership, and Anadarko. (In addition, make sure your stock holdings include at least one integrated oil company with a significant position in natural gas production, especially either Amoco or Unocal.)

Pure plays like the Hugoton producers should be treasured when they come along at an attractive price, for they allow you to focus your investment on a single segment of the natural gas business—production—without having to worry about the fate of a company's other businesses that could detract from its natural gas position and unduly hurt the stock's performance. I know from my perspective as an analyst who works with a variety of clients that investors automatically ask for the pure plays when they become excited about natural gas prospects. Thus, your investments in these Hugoton gems will be continually supported by future investors as they rush to establish their own stock positions when natural gas prices are moving higher.

Now is the time to invest in natural gas, a natural alternative to the country's increasing dependence on imported oil. At a time when energy resources in the U.S. are becoming more valuable than energy in the Middle East, we're self-sufficient in natural gas, and keeping it flowing doesn't require the protection of aircraft carriers, destroyers, battleships, minesweepers, and Marines.

18

Natural gas produced in the United States is actually in surplus now on a deliverability basis, creating the notorious gas "bubble" that has kept prices relatively depressed since 1985. Yet as this chronic gap between supply and demand finally tightens up, perhaps as early as the winter of 1987–88, economic factors and a bit of panic buying could send wellhead prices sharply higher and producer profits soaring.

Another reason I'm so confident about the ultimate prospects for Plains, Dorchester Hugoton, Mesa, and Anadarko is that they all offer a concentrated representation in long-lived natural gas reserves that are not being produced to capacity. Thus, by buying today when the price of natural gas is lagging behind oil's strong recovery, you can reap the present and anticipated value of these resources decades into the future, profiting from a number of high-priced cyclical peaks.

Compared to an industry average of about eleven years, Mesa has a reserve-life index of eighteen years, Dorchester twenty-one years, and Plains and Anadarko both twenty-two years. Buy these stocks for the long haul, confident that their stock prices will reflect many years of natural gas production when gas is worth much more than it is today.

THEME NUMBER THREE:
BUY UNDERVALUED INTEGRATED OIL COMPANIES, USING MY 'MCDEP' TECHNIQUE

As an investor, you'll do fine by using my first two themes to select choice stocks that will thrive in a strengthening price environment for oil and gas. But to maximize your investment odds and increase your opportunities to realize a higher overall return on your energy portfolio, you should employ "McDep," a technique I've developed over the past fifteen years (and will explain in detail in Chapter 3).

McDep is a statistical ratio that reveals the relative value of each oil and gas company I follow. Basically, the ratio is determined in two steps. First, I add a company's stock market valuation and debt. Second, I divide that number by the estimated value of its properties.

This gives me an objective, universal measurement that I can use to compare the value of individual companies— as reflected in their current stock prices—and groupings within the industry. Important disparities clearly stand out and lead to a number of my current recommendations.

For example, the composite McDep ratio is highest for trusts and partnerships and independent producers, which are focused on a single objective: production of their oil and gas reserves. The lowest McDep ratios tend to be found among the integrated companies, which too often are penalized by stock market investors because of their sheer corporate size and diversity.

Integrated oil companies are those that combine exploration and production with refining and marketing; they do everything from searching for new oil to selling the eventual refined products that help run your car. Managers at these companies think it's advantageous to own everything under one corporate umbrella, yet my research shows that Wall Street investors actually pay less—on a relative basis—for what they regard as an inefficient combination of resources.

This is the reason for my campaign to break these large outfits into smaller, more concentrated pieces such as trusts and partnerships, independent production companies, and refining/marketing operations. These new entities, trading on the stock exchange, would have a much greater combined value than the original parent company, clearly reflecting the underlying values that were trapped inside the integrated structure.

And hence one of my basic investment strategies: *Buy the stock of low-McDep integrated companies and then wait for the various changes that will bring out more of the company's true underlying value.* If we think of pure plays as gems, many integrated companies are high-grade ore with gems concealed.

A takeover attempt, of course, represents the most dramatic outside force to bring about these changes. Low-McDep companies such as Kerr-McGee, Unocal, Phillips, and Amerada Hess are small enough targets, while size doesn't necessarily insulate a struggling behemoth like Texaco. However, I prefer to emphasize more realistic restructuring steps such as stock buyback programs, sales of unrelated businesses, spinoffs, and creation of independent corporations and master limited partnerships for oil and gas properties.

Ideally, these streamlining efforts will turn raw, multibillion-dollar integrated companies into separate, independent pieces that have their own identifiable stock market value. Collectively, the original surviving company and the various new entities will be worth far more than the company's original stock price before restructuring—and they can all benefit from continually higher oil and gas prices.

If there is to be any economic justification for combining properties into a company, the McDep ratio should normally be greater than 1.0, thereby reflecting management's contributions. Yet as a value investor, I usually resist buying a well regarded company with a high McDep ratio because most of the good news is already reflected in the stock price and there's relatively little appreciation potential over the near term. Instead, I prefer to buy a more poorly regarded, low-McDep company with unappreciated asset values, and then hope that the situation will improve—through corporate changes and improving oil and gas prices.

Therefore, using McDep ratios, restructuring potential, and unrecognized asset values (particularly U.S. oil and gas reserves) as the primary criteria for buying an integrated company, you would want to pick from among the nine companies in Table 1. I'll go into greater detail about these companies and the McDep technique in later chapters, but briefly here's how to interpret the data in this table.

In the second column, I've given you a McDep ratio for each company using the current going rate for oil and gas in the ground at $8/bbl and $1.10/mcf. This gives us a consistent starting point, based on stock prices in the recent past.

However, since you want to look ahead as an investor, you should place greater emphasis on future appreciation potential, as measured by McDep ratios in the third column. Here I've projected oil and gas in the ground at $12/bbl and $1.50/mcf, reflecting values reached at the previous cyclical highs in 1980 and 1981.

Column four gives you the actual appreciation potential in these stocks, as represented by their projected present value of equity (also known as asset value or breakup value) under $12/$1.50 conditions. High-debt companies such as Unocal and Phillips are relatively more undervalued on that basis, benefiting from the financial leverage that debt provides in a rising market.

Finally, I compare current stock prices to projected prices in the fifth column, giving you stock appreciation potential on a percentage basis—the true bottom line.

TABLE 1.1 UNDERVALUED INTEGRATED OIL COMPANIES RANKED BY MCDEP

	PRICE 10/19 1987 ($/SH)	MCDEP RATIO (@$8/BBL)	MCDEP RATIO (@$12/BBL)	PROJECTED PRICE ($/SH)	STOCK APPRECIATION POTENTIAL (%)
Kerr-McGee	36	.77	.60	75	110
Phillips	11.8	.79	.60	45	280
Mobil	32	.74	.57	88	170
Unocal	29	.74	.56	102	250
Amerada Hess	23	.68	.53	62	170
Texaco	33	.66	.52	93	180
Chevron	41	.69	.52	112	170
Amoco	60	.62	.50	162	170
Sun	36	.58	.45	117	220

Whatever your investment time frame, the nine integrated companies in Table 1.1 are promising stock market plays. They are all relatively undervalued and, for various reasons (as I'll detail in Chapter 4), are either vulnerable to a takeover bid or under pressure to restructure their operations and bring out greater value to shareholders.

Moreover, these companies are well positioned to cash in on the rising value of their oil and gas reserves. Since the integrated group as a whole (seventeen companies) have 80 percent of the publicly owned U.S. oil and gas reserves, owning stock in several of these companies represents the best way to capitalize on booming energy prices in the years ahead.

BETTING ON THE INHERENT VALUE OF 'BLACK GOLD'

Oil Shock III—its inevitability and magnitude—will continue to be one of the most important, hotly debated economic concerns in this country for years to come, sustaining a fertile environment for oil and gas stocks. That's yet another reason why I feel you can buy the stocks featured in this book with conviction, based on the trends already in place and widespread fears about what the future could easily bring. Instead of simply waiting around for a potential energy disaster to happen, use this book to plot a strategy that will hedge your investment portfolio against these ominous trends. Start building positions in several of my recommended stocks that appear most appealing so that you can eventually profit from a belief most people embrace or are subliminally prepared to accept—

that the oil glut of 1986 and 1987 was only a temporary phenomenon and that inevitably oil prices once again will go through the roof, carrying energy stocks with them.

Even without an actual oil crisis, I'm optimistic that oil prices will continue to trend upward toward a major new cyclical peak in the years ahead, driven by inexorable supply-and-demand factors in the United States and around the world. Buy my recommended stocks with either prospect in mind, knowing that the *long-term* trends are in place, while restructuring efforts could bring short-term bonanzas to several of these recommended companies.

All the while, remember that history, economic trends, and human nature are all on your side when you bet on the irrefutable value of "black gold." Will Rogers was talking about another commodity, but he certainly could have meant oil when he said, "The best investment is land, because they ain't making any more of it."

CHAPTER 2

LESSONS TO BE LEARNED

How can I be so certain that events in the oil and gas business will unfold the way I've suggested?

History, for one thing, appears to be on my side. As Norman Cousins points out, "History is a vast early-warning system," and the events of the past twenty years should certainly warrant alarm about what lies ahead. But we can also be ready to seize the investment opportunities I'll be stressing in this book.

I've been fortunate that my own twenty-year career analyzing the oil and gas business has paralleled the most dynamic, explosive era in the industry's history. I've observed the genesis of two worldwide energy crises, the impact they had on stock market investments, and their ultimate resolution. I've also watched the inescapable power and momentum of supply-and-demand cycles as they move the world's oil market from periods of supply glut to supply shortages, and oil prices from multiyear peaks to multiyear lows.

Along the way, I've made my share of mistakes as an

analyst and as an investor, but I like to think I've learned a lot from these experiences and that I now have a valuable perspective on how we got here and how these past events will affect where we're now going.

My interest in energy stocks developed rather early, when I was still in junior high school in Grafton, Wisconsin, a rural community north of Milwaukee. Using money I had earned delivering newspapers and working on my uncle's farm, I invested in the stock market and proceeded to accumulate small amounts of shares in companies like Iowa Public Service, Northrop, and Hoffman Electronics. I also bought Cherokee Uranium, at my mother's urging, but the company proceeded to go bankrupt and I learned my first lasting lesson about investing: Avoid the "can't miss" high-flyers with exotic names but risky prospects.

After majoring in chemical engineering at the University of Wisconsin, I moved to San Francisco in 1963 to take a job as a refinery engineer with Chevron (then Standard Oil of California). Perhaps I would still be at Chevron today, a middling vice-president buried deep within that $35 billion company, had I not met Louise soon after my arrival. We got married about six months later, and it didn't take her long to notice that I wasn't bringing any work home from Chevron. She sensed—correctly—that I was in the wrong job at the wrong corporation, and urged me to enter Harvard Business School, which I did in 1965.

My first job after Harvard was with A. D. Little, the Cambridge consulting firm, where I worked on a wide range of energy-related projects for about four years. I helped present our research findings to clients and I also took calls from brokerage clients and money-management firms to discuss specific issues involving the oil and gas business. This all gave me a taste of what it was like to be a research analyst and led me to my job with Donaldson, Lufkin and Jenrette in July 1971.

THE EARLY WARNINGS OF OIL CRISIS NO. 1

When I joined DLJ, the Dow Jones industrial average stood at about 890, U.S. crude oil was selling for about $3.50 per barrel, and OPEC (the Organization of Petroleum Exporting Countries) was only beginning to assert itself as a cartel with power and unity.

Looking back, that was obviously an opportunistic time to break into my business, a full two years before Middle East warfare and the Arab oil embargo brought revolutionary changes to the world's energy market. Yet the early 1970s were far from a somnolent era as the United States began to wrestle—unsuccessfully—with major emerging energy problems and in the process set itself up as a prime target for an OPEC-inspired oil shock.

Basically, as we headed into 1970, the country's energy security was at the mercy of government officials and members of Congress who must have fallen asleep in science class the day the teacher discussed a fundamental law of physics: "Every action has a reaction." As a result, many years of price controls, oil import quotas, and other government regulations had undermined the U.S. oil and gas industry, leaving the country vulnerable to sudden shortages of energy supplies and unable to respond sensibly to inequities in the marketplace.

On the one hand, the government used oil import

quotas from 1957 onward to protect and encourage the domestic industry. These quotas artificially supported U.S. oil production at prices *above* the world price (about $3 per barrel versus $1 per barrel in 1970). On the other hand, natural gas prices were frozen at their mid-1950s level, despite the growing importance of gas as a primary energy source.

Over time, these "political economics" helped to create an energy fiasco. The unrealistically low prices for natural gas, especially in competition with U.S.-produced oil, stimulated demand for gas but discouraged replacement of supply; exploration simply didn't make economic sense. Inevitably, after years of abundant supply, natural gas shortages suddenly appeared among industrial users around the country, starting during the winter of 1969–70.

One contributing problem here was the status of natural gas as the cleanest of our conventional sources of energy at a time when the "clean air" movement was gathering momentum. Public utilities and industries, at the urging of the government and antipollution groups, were rapidly switching from oil and coal to natural gas. But the natural gas industry—crippled by years of price controls—was unable to respond to surging demands. This shifted greater demand to oil, but there was no spare capacity in domestic oil production to take up the slack; U.S. producers were pumping all the oil possible on a daily basis.

As a result, expanding U.S. energy demands—fueled by low-cost supplies, economic expansion, and population growth, while complicated by growing environmental concerns—led to a booming appetite for cheap oil imports.

Here's where OPEC members finally sensed their opening. Led by the Persian Gulf countries, whose governments were increasingly infiltrated by smart young people who had gone through U.S. business schools, the cartel began to capitalize on the realities of supply and demand. The Persian Gulf producers, who dominated world production and commanded well over half the world's proven reserves, perceived (1) that these reserves had a finite nature—especially if they were used to meet the ominous long-term trend in worldwide energy demand—and (2) that their oil was obviously worth much more than they were receiving on the world markets. So it made sense: Why shouldn't they charge more for it?

That's exactly what happened, starting in early 1971, when we saw the first real international power play by OPEC. After a series of threats to cut off oil supplies, and repeated warnings and confrontations, OPEC negotiated higher posted prices for Middle Eastern oil exports to the major international oil companies. Venezuela followed by immediately increasing prices to U.S. buyers by 25 percent. The "war," in effect, was on. The U.S. government had helped keep consumers happy with cheap energy throughout the 1960s, but now everybody would pay the price of those policies.

Through 1971 and 1972, worldwide consumption of petroleum products continued to grow at an alarming clip, and energy shortages became a major concern in the industrialized world. With consumption of all energy sources rising at a faster rate than population growth, some pessimists saw us in "a race for our lives to meet our energy demands" over the next three decades. One clear sign of these obvious strains came when President Nixon was forced to increase oil imports sharply in September 1972, as U.S. producers were unable to keep pace with demand.

Since sharply higher international prices had failed to deter this demand, Americans sent an encouraging message to OPEC that there was certainly more room for higher prices. If you can charge more for your product and still have demand go up, why not?

THE PIVOTAL YEAR: 1973

By year-end 1972, I saw enough emerging signs of an impending energy crisis that I titled my January research piece "The Oil and Gas Shortage of 1973." Moreover, I was so confident about the prospects for energy stocks that I felt they should account for 20 to 25 percent of a client's *total* portfolio. Indeed, many of these stocks had a spectacular year.

At the time, domestic crude oil prices continued to be supported above the cost of imports, but by April 1973, Middle Eastern crude had risen to $5 per barrel (bbl), compared to $3.50 per barrel (bbl) for domestic U.S. crude. This was a crucial reversal in prices and it created a new set of problems.

Basically, U.S. oil producers were no longer protected by an oil-import program, but would now be throttled by newly imposed government price controls on oil, enacted in response to steadily climbing international prices. We now had artificially low prices for U.S. crude oil production, which would help keep consumers and industrial users happy over the short-term but would ultimately cause financial hardships.

The American dream of an endless supply of low-cost energy was rapidly fading, but neither the administration nor Congress seemed willing to make the urgent changes I felt were necessary to rescue us from the impending energy squeeze. "Near-term energy shortages are unavoidable," I wrote, "and sources of energy supply are now strained to the limit at current prices." Thus, I argued that natural gas prices should be decontrolled and that domestic oil prices should be allowed to reach parity with the international price. Both steps would give producers an economic incentive to explore for new reserves of oil and gas, which then supplied 75 percent of our energy needs. I admitted there was strong political resistance to higher domestic oil and gas prices, no matter how justified the economic case might be, but the alternative would be a continually increasing flow of dollars to OPEC countries.

Our already severe fuel problems worsened in May 1973, when the Arabs began using oil as a diplomatic weapon and as a bargaining tool with the West in their continuing struggle against Israel. Four Arab countries—Algeria, Iraq, Kuwait, and Libya—temporarily halted oil shipments to the United States and other Western nations in protest against their support of Israel. Then when war broke out between Israel and the Arab countries in October, the Arabs embargoed all oil shipments to the United States and other nations.

Since the United States had expected the Middle East to supply the additional oil needed to meet growing U.S. energy needs—even at steadily higher prices—the embargo was a rude but necessary jolt, confronting Americans with some chilling realities but bringing about important and lasting efforts to conserve energy. In a nationwide address, President Nixon described the resulting energy shortage as the most serious the nation had faced since World War II, and when he later unveiled his plan for dealing with the emergency, he vowed, "As we look to the future, we can do so confident that the energy crisis will be resolved—not only for our time, but for all time."

Unfortunately, the president's plan failed to address a root cause of the entire problem: the continued regulation of oil and natural gas prices at artificially depressed levels. The oil embargo had dramatized why the United States needed to spur development of domestic energy resources, but federal price controls foreclosed all-out exploration and production efforts. As a result, I noted, American consumers were paying a higher price to Middle Eastern producing countries than to our own domestic producing companies—and, in effect, paying "billions in tribute" to help arm a dictator like Colonel Qaddafi in Libya.

Eventually, of course, regulatory actions had to give ground to more powerful underlying economic forces. Yet not until 1978 did natural gas legislation finally establish attractive incentives for natural gas exploration and development. Meanwhile, crude oil wellhead prices (the price of oil as it comes from the ground) remained regulated until January 1980. The average U.S. wellhead price had risen to $16 by that time, but was still just *half* the world level.

SEAT-OF-THE-PANTS INVESTMENT LESSONS

While these developments in the oil world were unfolding, I was gaining greater confidence in my ability to anticipate emerging investment themes and identify stocks within that theme with the best appreciation potential. Yet my experience with a stock that I was urging clients to *sell* actually best reinforced my sense of how important it was to be persistent with a good investment idea and not be easily swayed by dissenting voices.

I learned this lesson when I tangled with Coastal States Gas Corporation in 1972.

Starting in April, I began warning investors through my regular research commentary on the natural gas industry that with higher prices looming, Coastal States was overpriced at $50 a share and ought to be sold. I felt that Coastal, a pipeline company, faced an increasingly onerous burden of meeting large volume, long-term, fixed-price sales contracts that had been negotiated during the 1960s with large industrial and electrical utility customers. As current prices rose, the company would be squeezed to meet contractual requirements at these fixed lower rates.

Even with Coastal still strong at $48 a share in August, I reiterated my "sell" recommendation, adding my suspicion that Coastal had used dubious business practices to create an artificially high rate of growth and return.

Instead of continuing to bury my opinions about Coastal inside my general industry commentaries, I finally decided to write a full-blown company report in November. Unfortunately, I unwisely sent my drafted report to Coastal's investor relations person before writing the final report. I knew I was right about my conclusions, having researched the company while at A. D. Little and having followed up with several trips to company headquarters in Texas, but I thought it would be courteous to let management know in advance what I was going to say, since my report was quite negative.

I certainly gained their attention. Two days later, chairman Oscar Wyatt flew to New York with his lawyer and his investment bankers to meet with me, my boss, and our company's president. Mr. Wyatt said I didn't know what I was talking about and that if I published my work, it would damage important negotiations that were under

34

way with another company and could cause his company to go bankrupt!

Well, as a rookie analyst, I was sufficiently intimidated and I decided against publishing the full report. But I continued to sound my warnings and, as it developed, Coastal fared even worse than I anticipated. I had predicted that the company could go bankrupt with its fixed-price contracts in a couple of years, yet that very winter there were gas shortages in Texas and sharply higher prices, causing my projections to materialize almost instantly. Coastal stock plummeted from the mid-$30s in December to $6 a share in May, when the Securities and Exchange Commission suspended trading for six months.

I never took any great pleasure in this "sell" coup, except to know that my analysis had proved correct and that I had saved quite a few DLJ clients a lot of money by either chasing them out of the stock early or warning them away from even buying it. This experience also gave me greater confidence to be stubborn about my convictions in the future.

Another of the early lessons I learned about investing came when I recommended Eason Oil at $27 in 1972. This was my favorite among the small exploration companies that were concentrating on finding natural gas, spurred on by a Federal Power Commission decision a year earlier to allow a 30 to 50 percent increase in prices for new contracts between producers and distributors (pipeline companies). Despite my optimism that "exploration for natural gas is transforming from a stagnant industry to a major growth opportunity," Eason stock declined to $23 in August. I reiterated my recommendation, and ultimately it proved to be a successful idea when Eason was acquired by ITT for $78 a share in 1977. Like so many investors, though, I didn't stick with the Eason stock I owned as it rose those

50 points from the time of my recommendation. In fact, I sold at $18. Missing out on that ultimate profit certainly gave me much greater patience to stay invested in a company in which I had convictions about the eventual payoff in its underlying oil and gas properties. In subsequent years, a number of other recommended stocks have taken time to work out, but when I'm confident about the inherent property values, I find that they almost always prove ultimately quite rewarding.

THE TRANSITION BETWEEN ENERGY SHOCKS

The era between the Arab embargo in 1973 and the Iranian revolution in early 1979 provided a breather between energy shocks. In fact, world oil prices actually declined in real terms over that period, restrained by reduced energy demand (the result of continued high energy prices, a worldwide recession, and conservation efforts) and increasing supply from non-OPEC countries such as Mexico and the United Kingdom.

I continued to champion oil and gas stocks during these years, emphasizing their long-term investment potential but also employing an early version of my McDep technique.

One of my themes was that the development of new energy supplies had become an undisputed economic priority and this would help insure higher profitability for producers. Building on this rationale in May 1975, I compared all the independent natural gas exploration companies on an asset-value basis to isolate the most undervalued situations. This led to nine recommended companies as a way to capitalize not only on gas production but takeover potential. By 1980, the overall appreciation for these nine stocks had been spectacular for the patient investor, with six of the stocks succumbing to takeovers (Superior, Southland Royalty, General American, Supron, Aztec, and Dorchester Gas).

A major new theme also began to emerge in my 1974 research pieces as oil prices rose strongly but stock prices plunged during a severe recession, and this was the potential for financial restructuring among the integrated oil companies. The value of U.S. oil and gas reserves was steadily rising as domestic prices moved toward the world level as fast as regulation allowed, yet the stocks of integrated companies were selling far below their actual property value.

"The stock market offers the cheapest oil reserves," I argued. "Oil abounds on Wall Street at prices substantially lower than the cost of finding new supplies." An obvious strategy, I suggested, was that integrated companies ought to be buying back their own shares, since oil and gas reserves were cheaper on the New York Stock Exchange than in the ground.

I recommended a second approach to restructuring in September 1975 as an important way to enhance shareholder value. "If a Sun Oil were *dis*integrated into several independent refining/marketing companies," I wrote, "the sum of the parts would probably command greater market value than the whole." As we'll see throughout this book, that's a philosophy I'm still advocating today with many of the integrated companies.

OIL CRISIS NO. 2

The fragile nature of the world's oil market—and the ever-present danger of major oil-supply disruptions—took an ominous turn in October 1978 when internal political unrest halted Iran's extensive crude-oil production, thus eliminating most of the world's excess (spare) production capacity. A rapidly tightening crude-oil supply situation subsequently led to more aggressive pricing by major OPEC producers starting January 1, 1979.

The Iranian revolution soon followed, ousting the Shah and halting Iranian oil production for more than two months, thus removing over 5 million barrels per day off the world market. The ensuing scramble for petroleum led to panic oil buying and gave OPEC an unprecedented opportunity to escalate its prices with virtual disdain for the resulting impact on Western economies. Saudi Arabian crude, for example, moved up every quarter in 1979 and 1980, advancing from about $13 to an eventual top of $35 in 1981.

Most oil and gas stocks scored equally impressive gains over that period of time, reflecting the rising value of their proven reserves and anticipation of greater production at continually higher prices.

My most important investment criteria at that time, and an emphasis that continues to pay off today, was a belief in the *long-term value of U.S. oil and gas reserves*. Even in the troubled spring of 1979, I noted that domestic integrated companies were still selling for only about a third of their asset value in the stock market and that increasing investor respect for asset values would lead stock prices much higher.

In hindsight, of course, almost every energy-related

38

stock was a screaming buy through 1979 and most of 1980, until a speculative "blow-off" occurred in October and November. Yet many investors were continually reluctant to risk their money in oil and gas stocks. They worried that any tightness in world oil supply (such as occurred with the loss of Iranian production) would prove temporary and that the oil glut that existed in 1978 would eventually resume. Moreover, these skeptical investors argued that the world couldn't tolerate the existing high prices and that these prices would be coming down. Eventually they proved right, but not until 1981, and in the meantime they missed a spectacular bull market in these energy-related stocks.

Ironically, the final buying frenzy for oil and gas stocks came during a world oil surplus, estimated at as much as 2.5 million barrels per day. But this glut proved rather meaningless when war broke out between Iran and Iraq in September 1980, halting oil exports that had been averaging 3.7 million barrels per day, or about 10 percent of the world's supply. Prices on the spot market (where petroleum was not committed to long-term contracts) subsequently leaped from $31 to more than $40 as certain countries had to scramble to find new supplies.

SOWING THE SEEDS OF DESTRUCTION

Gradually but inexorably, higher oil prices in the 1970s created conditions that would ultimately prove more powerful than any governmental efforts to control the energy markets. OPEC was obviously dominant in 1979 ("A Cartel That Has World By The Throat," according to one headline writer at the time), but overplayed its hand and actually sowed the seeds of destruction by pushing oil prices to an artificially high level. These actions led to $10 oil instead of $50 oil.

The conditions I've cited, embodied in classic supply-and-demand cycles, set the stage for today's investment opportunities while leaving us with the specter of yet another oil crisis. So let's look at the basic economic responses that were triggered by OPEC's aggressive oil-pricing action, for they will help you interpret the current pricing cycle as it heads upward from its mid-1986 low toward a new multiyear peak in the years ahead.

First, *higher prices finally broke the rising demand trend for oil and gas*. For one thing, they led to worldwide economic slowdowns in 1974–75 and 1981–82, thus curbing demand by a significant amount. Meanwhile, energy shocks and higher prices made further inroads on demand by helping to inspire important conservation efforts in the industrial countries. Gradually, citizens and industry alike shifted to alternative fuels or found ways to use less—for example, by buying cars that got twenty miles per gallon instead of ten and building homes and offices that were more energy efficient. The high prices enforced by OPEC challenged consumers to use less or find alternatives, which finally caused energy demand to peak in 1979 and head downward.

Second, *higher prices* (coupled with major new oil discoveries in the non-OPEC world) *caused an eventual surplus of supply as higher-cost exploration and production became economically feasible*. The opening of the great Prudhoe Bay field in Alaska, Mexico's emergence as a major world producer, and successful North Sea exploration added billions of barrels of oil reserves by mid-1975, while new production brought 7 million to 8 million barrels per day of non-OPEC oil into the market.

In the United States, for example, price controls on new oil were lifted in September 1975, allowing higher domestic oil prices and inspiring aggressive capital spending on new crude-oil supply—not only to turn a profit but to lessen U.S. dependency on OPEC oil production.

All this enthusiasm for spending billions of dollars to find and develop new oil and gas reserves helped contribute to a world glut in 1979 and 1980, alleviated only by revolution and warfare in the Middle East, as I pointed out earlier. In the United States, for example, imports fell to their lowest level in five years while drilling for oil and gas reached its highest level in almost twenty-five years.

Overproduction by OPEC members themselves also contributed to a substantial surplus of oil inventories. When prices were soaring, these countries began expensive development projects and borrowed heavily. But then when conditions supporting these high prices began to erode and prices began declining in the 1980s, OPEC members were spurred to produce even more oil to earn the hard currency needed to meet their financial obligations. And very simply, the more they produced, the more they caused the eventual collapse of prices, from $28 per barrel in early December 1985 to $10 in mid-1986. (While stock prices for most energy-related companies peaked in late 1980, oil prices themselves didn't top out until about six months later, and then only declined gradually until their eventual nose-dive.)

INEFFICIENT INVESTMENTS BY MANY INTEGRATED OIL COMPANIES

Flush with surging cash flows in the late 1970s, most U.S. integrated oil companies not only embarked on ambitious exploration and production programs, but also poured billions of dollars into diversification efforts and expansion of their refining and marketing outfits. In both instances—diversification and integration—the investments spawned many unwieldy, inefficient companies that were ill-prepared for the takeover craze between 1981 and 1984. A half dozen of these companies failed to survive and several of the survivors still remain undervalued investment opportunities today, as pinpointed by my McDep technique.

Back in those fat-cat days for the oil industry, diversification reflected an attitude of the times—the conglomerate era—but also a desire by the managements of most integrated companies to lessen their dependence on the cyclical fortunes of oil and gas. After many lean years, these managements had become greatly overcapitalized (a combination of low debt and strong cash flow), but instead of using this financial strength to benefit shareholders by repurchasing stock and investing in oil and gas production properties, they went on a buying binge outside the energy business. Even Exxon got carried away, buying into the office equipment industry, while others invested in minerals, particularly the copper industry. Managers thought they were buying cheap at the bottom of the copper industry's cycle for a long-term profit, but the copper business slumped even lower after they all bought in. Over the years, Standard of Ohio (now wholly owned by British

Petroleum) sunk about $4 billion into copper and eventually had to write off their investment. Atlantic Richfield had a similar disaster with Anaconda, and Amoco wasted several billions on its Cyprus Minerals operation.

Meanwhile, excess cash flow was also being funneled into upgrading and expanding refining operations—what I've long regarded as a low-return business as compared to exploration and production. Quite predictably, with so many companies trapped into investing in refining in order to remain competitive, the industry was swamped with capacity just when oil prices peaked and triggered a sharp decline in demand. The resulting excess of refining capacity lasted until 1986.

PROFITING FROM THE TAKEOVER CRAZE

With hindsight, we know that most energy-related stocks hit their historic peaks in October and November of 1980. Yet my monthly report on January 5, 1981, asked the question, "Can the energy stocks do it again in 1981?"

Even after their powerful advances the previous two years (a 60 percent median gain in each year for the ten domestic integrated companies), I still felt that a number of companies remained "fundamentally undervalued." This judgment was based heavily on my traditional technique: comparing a company's stock price to the present value of its oil and gas reserves, and then isolating those companies with low ratios.

I also reminded my clients that drilling for oil and gas on the stock exchange was still cheaper than drilling in the ground. Therefore, I suggested that large integrated companies might soon shift their search for reserves to the smaller integrated companies, which remained quite cheap by historical and absolute standards. These undervalued reserves also highlighted restructuring possibilities that management could then use to bring out greater values for shareholders and stave off a potential takeover attempt.

By emphasizing takeover/restructuring candidates among the small integrated companies—and isolating the most likely targets—I had found an investment theme that would enable investors to nail down sizable gains in the oil group at a time when most energy-related stocks were underperforming the stock market.

Marathon Oil was the spark that got this trend rolling (although Conoco actually succumbed first, in a takeover by DuPont). I had recommended the company since 1975, citing its enormous untapped value and wondering when management would take restructuring steps to bring out that value for shareholders. Otherwise the company was vulnerable to a takeover bid, as I stressed in my buy recommendation on April 1, 1981, when the stock was $55 a share—well below its fifty-two-week high of $82.

I suggested, for example, that volatile refining and marketing operations were hurting Marathon's stock and should be split off from the exploration and production unit; failing to make an unconventional move like that could cost the company its independence.

A company spokesman objected to my proposal, saying, "We don't believe the (divestiture) approach is in the best long-term interests of our shareholders." But as management later discovered, slavish adherence to "integration is good" is not always in the long-term best interest of management. Marathon stock dropped as low as $49 in June that year, but Mobil started a bidding war in

October by offering $85 a share. U.S. Steel eventually acquired the company for $105 a share in December.

After Cities Service was swallowed up by Occidental in August 1982, I began emphasizing Phillips, Sun, and Getty Oil as "the next best investments among U.S. integrated companies."

I had been promoting Getty's many virtues for several years and began citing its takeover vulnerability in December 1981, when I focused on the search for "the next Marathon." Getty stock was $69 at that point and would sink as low as $41 in 1982, but I kept it on my recommended list. I'm infinitely patient when I feel I have a good investment idea that will eventually pay off.

Getty stock was widely shunned at the time, held down by its extreme sensitivity to oil prices at a time when investors feared a decline in those prices. Many investors also felt that Getty's potential appeal was complicated by concentrated ownership. Half of Getty's stock was held by two holders, the Sarah Getty Trust with 39 percent and the J. Paul Getty Museum with 11 percent, and it would be impossible to gain control of the company without concurrence by one of those stockholders.

In April 1982, after the stock had slumped to $48, I wrote, "Getty's stock is so cheap that shareholders have to ask why they are not realizing more value." Not at all shy about giving free advice, I suggested that management could enhance shareholder value by repurchasing stock, spinning off refining/marketing operations, and creating a royalty trust or limited partnership with part of the company's crude-oil operations. "Otherwise shareholders are likely to continue realizing only a fraction of the value of the properties behind the stock."

Getty management vigorously opposed restructuring and even dismissed the existence of value disparities. When the stock rallied to $60—or *half* the ultimate takeover price—the chairman of Getty said that estimates of Getty's true property value were "highly speculative," and that analysts making these judgments about the company's worth didn't know what they were talking about.

Gordon Getty obviously disagreed. In May, J. Paul Getty's 49-year-old son had become the sole trustee of the Sarah Getty Trust, giving him full control of about $1.5 billion worth of Getty stock for the first time. He was also a trustee of the Getty Museum and a director of Getty Oil Company, which in my estimation made him "the most important individual stockholder in the oil and gas business."

In December, sensing that Gordon Getty was likely going to become more active with his concentrated ownership of Getty stock, I reiterated my buy recommendation. The stock was still just $49 a share. I emphasized the "compelling value of properties," the "huge annual cash flow generation," an "unusually low level of debt," and "the promise of structural change." By any measure, Getty was a cheap stock—the most undervalued among U.S. integrated companies.

Gordon Getty had been reading my research reports on the company, and in January we had a meeting in San Francisco to discuss further my notions of how to increase the value of Getty stock. He never committed himself as I laid out my case, but I was encouraged by his obvious interest in enhancing value for shareholders and I was impressed by how well he grasped the situation and the possibilities. Knowing that he *understood* what we were talking about, I was confident that he had enough common sense to pursue some of those ideas.

Even then, I had to continue waiting patiently until October 1983, when Gordon Getty began openly opposing management and sought to take more active control of the company. Then came the long-rumored takeover bid in December, when Pennzoil offered $100 a share for 20 percent of Getty. I advised clients that the final price for Getty would more likely be $120 a share and there could be a bidding battle.

Sure enough, Texaco snatched the company away from Pennzoil with an eventual $128 offer, which would later embroil the companies in their historic $10 billion lawsuit.

FROM TAKEOVER TARGETS TO RESTRUCTURING CANDIDATES

After Gulf Oil was acquired by Chevron in April 1984, the takeover era was clearly on the wane; many of the major oil companies were digesting an acquisition and most of the vulnerable targets were no longer independent. So I widened my investment focus to the restructuring potential (e.g., stock buybacks, spinoffs, and divestitures) at eight or ten integrated companies, regardless of their size or actual takeover potential. Most of these companies remain on my recommended list (as we'll see in Chapter 4), in anticipation of favorable company developments and the long-term trends I see in place for oil prices.

Always remember, as we go through this book and as you build a portfolio of energy-related stocks, that the oil and gas business is inevitably cyclical and rarely progresses along a smooth trend line in either direction. Production decisions by the major producing countries and warfare among these nations can obviously have dramatic short-term influences on crude oil prices.

47

Yet as unpredictable as oil might appear to be as a commodity, the forces of supply and demand lead to clearly defined peaks and valleys in oil prices that stand out when seen with a multiyear perspective. Every major peak in prices (as we saw in 1980–81) generates greed and excesses that cause the upward cycle to self-destruct, and these conditions—over time—help create an eventual new cyclical bottom (as we saw in mid-1986). Subsequently, these cyclical lows recreate the conditions that lead to yet another peak, which is where we're headed now.

As we progress through 1988, I'm confident we can anticipate a continued upward cycle in oil and gas prices, building from the $18 base established by OPEC in the first half of 1987 and moving ever higher. Knowing what I know about the energy business and what I've observed over the past twenty years, the U.S. is growing increasingly vulnerable to yet another energy crisis. I'd be foolhardy to predict *when* this might happen, but in the meantime, you can use this book to start making money over the near-term in specific oil and gas stocks. We'll lay the groundwork by gaining a better understanding of my McDep technique in Chapter 3.

CHAPTER 3

HOW TO LEARN TO LOVE THE MCDEP RATIO

Wall Street analysts all learn to develop their own individualized methods for evaluating and comparing the many companies they follow. Most of my oil and gas colleagues emphasize future earnings prospects, though some go an important step further and highlight anticipated cash flow, a more accurate measuring tool.

I prefer to rely on my McDep technique, which I feel I've refined into the most reliable method available for determining the true value of a company with more than 10 percent of its property value in U.S. oil and gas reserves. By crunching my financial data about a company into one number—the McDep ratio—I can (1) rank companies in terms of their relative value as stock market investments, and (2) objectively spotlight those stocks that should best capitalize on the coming trends stressed in this book.

The basic technicalities of McDep are reasonably simple, so let's go through the key steps I take to yield a McDep ratio for a particular company. This should give you a greater appreciation for why you can rely on the McDep technique to identify the most undervalued oil and gas companies, especially as we look ahead several years. The more confidence you have in my analytical technique, the more conviction you will have about my investment conclusions and recommendations (even without calculating and updating McDep yourself).

The McDep ratio itself stands for market capitalization ("Mc") plus debt ("De") over property ("p"), or:

$$\frac{\text{Market cap + debt}}{\text{Property}} = \text{McDep}$$

Several years ago I found myself saying these components so often that one day it just came out as "McDep."

We derive the *numerator* by adding a company's stock market capitalization and debt. Using Amoco as the example (as of October 19, 1987), "market cap" is simply price ($60) times shares outstanding (260 million), which gives us $15.6 billion. Next we add debt of $8 billion, which is primarily long-term debt, but also includes other liabilities such as deferred taxes and preferred stock. (Beginning on page 195 in the Appendix, you will find a detailed explanation of how I obtain and calculate the many components of McDep, such as property values, reserve figures, and cash flow.)

Adding market cap and debt, our numerator becomes $23.6 billion. This is the value Wall Street investors and lenders place on the company—what they are willing to pay for Amoco's collection of assets. The numerator provides an objective measurement of any company, since it represents the collective judgment of many people

50

buying and selling that company's stock and debt every day.

The *denominator* of McDep is more subjective, for it represents my estimate of total property value. Basically, this is what I think the various parts of Amoco—the oil and gas reserves, the refineries, the service stations, the chemical plants, and other assets—would be worth if they were sold piecemeal to other companies or spun off as independent entities in the stock market. I valued Amoco's property at $38 billion, based on oil valued at $8/bbl in the ground and gas at $1.10 per thousand cubic feet (mcf) (when oil was selling for about $20 on the world spot markets).

Now we can do the math, taking the numerator (23.6 billion) and dividing by the denominator (38 billion), which gives us a McDep ratio of .62 for Amoco—lowest of all the large integrated oil companies.

Just as stock market investors give precise value to a company's stock at any given moment, the McDep technique enables me to reduce all my relevant data to one number. Using data from annual and quarterly reports, my own statistical judgments, and two computers, I come up with a single number that I can use to measure comparative value, not only among individual oil and gas companies but between their respective groupings. McDep measures all these companies by the same criteria (without factoring in quality of management) and thus highlights those that are relatively more undervalued.

This in turn helps narrow your investment focus and allows you to concentrate your subsequent research on the most promising situations.

PUTTING MCDEP TO WORK

Ideally, a company's McDep ratio should be at least 1.0 or greater, representing a balance between equity value and property value. Otherwise, what contribution is management making to enhance the value of the properties by reinvesting cash flow? Why have a company if the management can't produce a stock market value greater than the pieces they're working with?

In reality, as you can see by scanning Tables 1B–5B in the Appendix, McDep ratios can have a wide range— from .58 to 1.78—and herein lie valuation gaps that you can exploit as an investor.

The most obvious and important focal point of McDep is the integrated oil group, comprising twenty companies that own about 80 percent of the publicly held oil and gas reserves in the United States. Obviously, any meaningful investment in the energy business must include several of these integrated stocks.

You will notice that the small integrateds have a composite McDep of .73 at the current going rate and the large integrateds are .78, for a composite of .77—lower than all the other groups. There are half a dozen obvious low-McDep candidates here, thanks to the fact that publishing deadlines forced us to use stock prices as of October 19, 1987—Meltdown Monday, when the Dow Jones average plunged 508 points. Only a month or two earlier, however, most McDep ratios were considerably higher, and my clients were beginning to wonder, "Where's the deep undervaluation?"

I had to admit, there weren't many obvious you-can't-pass-this-up type of bargains in the oil and gas sector, thanks to the strong run-up by most stocks in late 1986 and continuing well into 1987. Higher oil prices and repeated crisis conditions in the Persian Gulf region (somewhat the exact scenario I'm anticipating into the 1990s) kept forestalling the profit-taking season. Yet I certainly never lost faith in McDep. I knew that as oil and gas prices trended upward, energy stocks would still have their inevitable corrections while marching higher and that McDep would continue to be a crucial investment ally in the search for buying opportunities.

If energy stocks have made a strong recovery from their mid-October lows, the key is to simply broaden McDep's horizon by looking further down the road. Continue to use it as a comparative technique among the more low-McDep integrated companies with restructuring potential, but learn to appreciate how it also emphasizes companies with impressive commodity potential in an environment of steadily rising oil and gas prices.

Recognizing that McDeps have indeed improved since mid-1986, particularly at integrated oil companies, I've adjusted by creating two sets of valuation tables that you can use in several ways.

1. MCDEP IN TODAY'S MARKET

One set of valuation tables is tied to the current going rate for oil and gas in the ground ($8/bbl and $1.10/mcf). You can calculate current McDep ratios off these tables (beginning on page 204 of the Appendix) by simply plugging in today's stock price for a particular company and assuming that the other McDep components are still valid. I've based my property estimates on a *sustained* oil price of about $18 to $20 on the crude-oil market through 1987. These prices would have to move up to a *sustained* level around $22 to

$24 before I would have to raise my values for oil and gas in the ground. (Always keep in mind that the moment I factor these higher values into my property estimates, McDep ratios automatically come down, reflecting the fact that stock prices haven't yet moved up to reflect increased underlying values. Over time, in a bullish environment, these McDep ratios will improve along with stock prices until world crude-oil prices once again dictate an even higher going rate for oil and gas in the ground.)

Current McDep ratios are still the most reliable way to compare the relative value of companies within a particular grouping (e.g., trusts and partnerships, independent oil and gas producers, diversifieds, pipelines, and integrateds). My strategy has been that if a McDep of 1.0 represents a company's actual value, then a company with a McDep of .90 has greater stock appreciation *potential* than a similar company with a McDep of 1.10, all things being equal.

This means, for example, that if you intended to buy a blue-chip oil company today, Amoco ($60/.62 McDep) should prove to be a more rewarding long-term investment than Exxon ($34/.82) or British Petroleum ($60/1.02). Projecting out to about 1990 (as I'll soon explain), I calculate $162 in present value of equity for Amoco, while Exxon improves to only $58 and British Petroleum manages to reach just $83.

2. MCDEP IN 1990

The first set of tables (beginning on page 196 in the Appendix) is based on my conviction that we should be reaching historic price highs in 1990, with oil and gas valued in the ground at $12/bbl and $1.50/mcf, as they were in 1980–81. These calculations give an exciting indication of the appreciation potential for many energy stocks and should help you invest with a confident long-term focus.

In fact, on the assumption that we'll be moving closer to $12 oil in the ground in 1988 and away from $8 oil, you should emphasize my $12/$1.50 tables in the Appendix as you use McDep to monitor energy stocks. That way you need not worry about updating property value estimates for existing oil and gas reserves, since I've already anticipated and calculated those future values. Simply plug in current stock prices and then focus your attention on the companies with the lowest McDep ratios, for they are the most undervalued stocks today in relation to those future projections. These are the stocks that stand to gain the most as oil and gas prices continue their upward trend.

Looking at these 1990-era tables, particularly for integrated companies and independent producers, you may wonder why some of them have different McDep rankings with $8 oil as compared to $12 oil. The reason is that each company will benefit in varying degrees from higher oil and gas prices. For example, certain heavy oil deposits will become economical to produce, and other high-cost production can be brought on stream, benefiting certain companies more than others. Stronger natural gas prices also will have a proportionately higher impact on those producers with significant long-life reserves. My future estimates also allow for some erosion in the reserves themselves, thus penalizing to a greater degree companies with short-life reserves.

An important column in my tables is a listing of "present value of equity" for each company using both $8/bbl and $12/bbl pricing conditions. Present value of equity is also called "asset value," or "breakup value." It is what a company's properties would be worth if sold in small pieces to other corporations, assuming that the going rate for oil and gas in the ground is consistent with the assumptions used in making the estimate. In my work, a McDep of 1.0 equals present value of equity, so when I look at potential future stock prices, I assume that each company will eventually have a McDep of 1.0. The gap between today's McDep ratio—as calculated using current stock prices—and that eventual McDep of 1.0 represents the stock's potential appreciation. If this seems overly optimistic for some stocks, keep in mind that a number of integrated companies had McDeps of 1.0 or higher at the current going rates in late August 1987. We can certainly anticipate a similar performance at the going rate in 1990.

When you begin to evaluate a group of stocks, make sure you take into account present value of equity, for it will help you bring comparative values into much clearer focus. For instance, when you update McDeps for any group of companies and compare present value of equity, the long-term bargains should clearly stand out (before taking into account more subjective factors about specific companies). If a stock is already near a McDep of 1.0 using our future pricing assumptions, I wouldn't want to invest in that stock. A British Petroleum at .82 might improve from $60 to $83 in this time frame, but a Unocal at .56 could leap from $29 to $102 with the same industry conditions.

MCDEP VALUATIONS CAN BE TRUSTED

McDep calculations inevitably are sensitive to assumptions (since no one has inside information on every company), but McDep is rarely far off as an indicator of equity value, based on my property value estimates. One objective test of the McDep technique is the price of corporate acquisitions, and since 1985, eight deals involving McDep companies have averaged a McDep of 1.0.

In April 1987, for example, British Petroleum's $74-a-share bid for Standard Oil equaled my most recent estimated present value of equity, published in my monthly publication shortly before the announced offer. For those investors who were relying on McDep at the time, an obvious implication of the Standard Oil takeover was that other integrated companies also should have been selling close to a current McDep of 1.0, reflecting the actual value of their properties—as endorsed by British Petroleum.

The closer you are in time to when I updated my $12/$1.50 tables for this book (October 19, 1987), the more you can rely on my McDep components without necessarily updating major developments at each company you're studying. Circumstances for each company tend not to change much each quarter, but you should keep your eye out for the kinds of changes that can affect McDep calculations—namely, a stock split, which creates more shares, and a major acquisition or discovery, which affects debt levels and proven reserves. A publication like *Value Line* can help keep you updated on most of the companies I feature.

HOW MCDEP CAN HELP IMPROVE YOUR INVESTMENT SUCCESS

Since the McDep technique highlights undervalued stocks, the investment opportunity might seem obvious: Buy the lowest McDep companies and then wait for developments to bring out that underlying value for stockholders.

With rare exceptions, this has been my basic strategy toward integrated oil companies in recent years, but no successful investment system is quite that easy or clear-cut across the board. While McDep serves as an excellent starting point for finding prime buying candidates, it should not be regarded as an all-purpose "buy" signal for every low-McDep company you uncover in my universe of one hundred stocks. Outside the integrated oil group, especially, you must supplement McDep with extra research in order to avoid companies that could prove risky, unreasonable investments, especially in comparison to the many stocks I'll be recommending in this book. After all, a low McDep indicates a company that's out of favor with investors and you should look for the possible reasons why. (Please check page 243 in the Appendix for a brief listing of the stocks I would consider avoiding, should they have an appealing McDep ratio.)

When you invest in the stock market, statistical techniques can be overemphasized but cannot be ignored if you intend to minimize the risks while maximizing the potential profits. I feel that the McDep technique is a proven way to accomplish those two goals and can help you become a successful long-term investor in oil and gas stocks. Here are some of the reasons why it's a treasured pal:

1. *McDep helps narrow your initial list of stocks in an objective, statistical manner.*

    After updating the McDep ratios for each company in the particular group that interests you (e.g., the oil and gas producers) and creating your own ranking list, you can now focus on the most intriguing targets and begin your follow-up research.

    Remember, the McDep ratio for any given

company is distilled from the opinions of investors and my analytical work, all reduced to a single number. This number gives you a sense of the company's relative value. You may not immediately know if $33 for Texaco is a good price to pay for Texaco relative to other integrated oil stocks, but a McDep ratio of .66 near the bottom of the group— tells you that the company is significantly undervalued and certainly worthy of further investigation.

The McDep technique is especially useful for studying oil and gas companies because the industry is capital intensive and relatively invulnerable to obsolescence. This means that capital investment is management's most important contribution to the company's success. At least in the eyes of investors, oil and gas reserves have a readily definable value that can be measured by McDep, independent of the management that controls those values. By contrast, McDep would be far less effective at valuing a company in a labor-intensive industry such as textiles, where people are far more important than the fixed assets and where management's crucial contribution is to manage employees and make sure they work efficiently. While McDep can measure the present and future value of an oil well in Texas, it won't tell you anything about labor relations at a textile company in North Carolina.

2. *McDep will help you invest in companies with the greatest potential for relative stock market appreciation in the years ahead.*

The lower the McDep, the more intrigued I become as I track one hundred stocks through McDep analysis. Low-McDep companies have more room for improvement and have the most to gain by changes, whether as a result of restructuring, a takeover, improving industry conditions, or regulatory changes (e.g., price deregulation in the natural gas business, as we've seen with one of my favorite small companies, Dorchester Hugoton). The more undervalued companies, as measured by McDep, are already poorly regarded in most cases and usually do not suffer much if news developments are negative, but they can benefit proportionately more if news developments are especially positive.

I'm sometimes going for the home run a bit more than most Wall Street analysts by often recommending out-of-favor companies such as Texaco and Amerada Hess and Mobil. But if my targeted stock can appreciate 70 percent in two years—by moving from, say, $30 to $51—that's still an enviable 30 percent gain a year (before commissions). Taking this perspective helps give me the patience I often need to stick with my "buy" recommendations until they ultimately pay off in a big way.

3. *Buy a low-McDep company with significant oil and gas reserves and you pay a discount for these reserves, giving your investment an extra dividend.*

For example, if the present value for oil in the ground is $8 bbl and you buy Amoco stock at a McDep of .62, you theoretically buy the company's oil reserves for a six-tenths discount, or $4.80 a barrel, and that should prove to be an attractive long-term commitment.

4. *By updating McDep ratios on a regular basis (basically taking into account stock price changes), you can track the relative attractiveness of companies within a particular group and spot favorable buying and selling opportunities.*

60

This will help you make more consistent, sensible decisions as you add new stocks to your portfolio or increase your position in a particular stock. For example, early in 1987, the higher McDep companies such as Exxon, British Petroleum, and Royal Dutch/Shell made powerful moves that widened the gap between them and the lower McDep companies such as USX, Unocal, Amerada Hess, and Texaco. The latter stocks moved up slightly in price but were still excellent buying opportunities within the McDep framework, as borne out by their subsequent upside moves.

When oil stocks are on a roll, McDep can also help you isolate a specific laggard. At one point in November 1986, takeover speculation had boosted USX and Amerada Hess past the prices some of my clients wanted to pay, so I looked for a similar company that I felt was vulnerable to restructuring yet more undervalued. Unocal, at $23 at the end of October (and with a McDep of .77), looked quite attractive on that basis. Indeed, it reached $33 by February and $45 in July.

5. *McDep can help you sense when to sell a winning stock.*

Just as you want to buy the lower McDep companies in a particular group, you should start thinking about selling once your stock moves past a McDep of 1.0—unless (1) there's an active outside investor who appears to be accumulating stock or has already announced a major stake in the company, thus putting the stock into play as a takeover/restructuring candidate, or (2) oil prices keep moving up, carrying all the energy stocks higher, even past seemingly overpriced levels.

(When I talk about stocks with a McDep of 1.0 in this context, I'm basing these calculations on a going rate of $8/$1.10 for oil and gas in the ground. If you're concerned that perhaps oil on the spot market now justifies a higher going rate in the ground—thus affecting my estimated property values and your McDep calculations—here's a good checkpoint: Determine a composite McDep ratio for about six or eight of the largest trusts and partnerships. If this composite is above 1.10 or 1.15, then conditions may be dictating a going rate of $9 a barrel for oil in the ground and I would simply start emphasizing my 1990 tables.)

When the two bullish scenarios I've just cited are missing, then selling a high-McDep winner and reinvesting in a low-McDep laggard is a good ongoing strategy. For example, I published a research report on USX in mid-June 1986, when the stock was $21 and had a McDep of .77. I argued that the properties of USX could trade in the stock market for a combined value of $37 a share if diversification and integration were reduced sufficiently (the $37 representing a McDep of 1.0). A year later, after the company had survived a takeover attempt by Carl Icahn and sold off its chemicals operation (now a high-flying stock, Aristech), USX reached a fifty-two-week high of $38¾. With little apparent upside potential remaining, unless investors were willing to gamble on a continued rebound by USX steel operations, I advised clients to sell if they wished—and to move into a more attractive McDep company such as Unocal (then $41), Kerr-McGee ($39), Texaco ($47), or Amoco ($84).

6. *Use McDep to avoid* overvalued *stocks.*

In order to make your investment capital grow over time, learning to sense what stocks to avoid can be as important as knowing what to buy, so be wary of companies with unusually high McDeps (beyond about 1.20). Even if you're in love with a company's fundamentals, a premium McDep should raise the caution flag—at today's stock price—and encourage you to be patient; profit-taking may eventually bring the stock down into a better buying range, but if not, there's always another good idea worth pursuing.

An investment in companies with McDeps between about 1.0 and 1.15 should be regarded more as an expression of confidence in the management than as a play on undervalued properties. While a well-managed company can certainly offer reassurance if you want a greater sense of security in your investment, paying too high a price (as measured by McDep) can limit your potential stock price appreciation and inject the risk of a near-term correction from these lofty heights.

Along these same lines, when you calculate McDep by using current stock prices and my $12/$1.50 tables, the closer any stock comes to a McDep of 1.0 as we look down the road several years, the less anxious you should be about buying at present prices.

7. *One important reason why you should use my 1990 target tables is that they already account for anticipated increases in property values, thus negating any need for you to update the going rate for oil and gas in the ground.*

This means that you can put McDep to work as

soon as you read this book, not having to worry if my current tables (based on oil and gas at $8/$1.10) are still valid measurements. By using my $12/$1.50 tables to calculate your McDep ratios for individual companies, any deviations from those listed in this book will be obvious and the disparities between companies quite clear.

Any stock with a notably lower McDep ratio today has to be of some interest, especially if most every other stock in its group has gone up, leaving it resting near the bottom of the group's McDep ratios. Conversely, if a low-McDep stock that I've emphasized in this book has made a strong move and is now in the middle of the group or even higher, you should be less interested—at current prices. But stay in touch with the stock's progress, for it may once again represent a bargain purchase, especially if my rationale for liking the stock remains relatively unchanged.

That's the whole purpose of McDep, to help you differentiate value in comparable stocks so that you can buy the right stock at lower prices. I'll be giving you a handle on about twenty favorite stocks in different areas of the oil and gas business, and now you can use McDep to judge for yourself whether the appeal is still there, using today's stock prices but projecting 1990 property values.

Ultimately, I find that McDep analysis lends conviction to my idea-oriented conclusions about specific companies. The McDep technique helps me remain focused on long-term, underlying values and thus keeps me from being easily distracted by short-term swings in the price of oil. In fact, perhaps out of principle, I've resisted buying a stock quotation machine for my office desk so that I'm not unduly influenced by daily stock market action. I want to stay the course with my recommended stocks until I feel they've fulfilled the potential highlighted by McDep.

CHAPTER 4

INTEGRATED OIL COMPANIES— RESERVES AND RESTRUCTURING

By spotlighting undervalued stocks that are selling on Wall Street for less than their property values, the McDep technique leads us straight to the integrated oil group—and many of the most promising investment opportunities in this book. I'll detail my current favorites later in the chapter and provide insights that should help you recognize other attractive buying situations. But first let's cover some important groundwork so you can more easily share my enthusiasm for certain integrated oil companies.

THE IMPORTANCE OF RESTRUCTURING AT INTEGRATED COMPANIES

Even as steadily rising oil prices and persistent Middle East tensions push integrated oil stocks to increasingly higher prices, tremendous underlying values remain trapped within the integrated corporate structure. This is especially evident when we look ahead and calculate McDep ratios based on oil and gas in the ground valued at $12/bbl and $1.50/mcf, their former cyclical highs of 1980–81 (see Table 4.1).

Yet while I'm a patient investor, willing to buy and hold the stocks I like until anticipated developments eventually unfold, I also know that the managements of integrated oil companies can hasten a realization of underlying values by restructuring their operations. But they need to be pushed, as I've tried to do in recent years by campaigning on behalf of shareholders through my monthly publication, speeches, and appearances at annual meetings.

One ongoing theme has been to encourage managements to correct what I've termed the "three sins"—diversification, integration, and sheer size—by turning their corporations into smaller, independent pieces through divestitures and spinoffs. As we've seen in the McDep rankings, these new, well-focused entities would tend to have McDep ratios close to 1.0 when freed of the integrated structure. And, collectively, they would deliver far more stock market value to shareholders of the original corporation.

The three "sins" have long caused investors to penalize the stock price of most integrated companies, as reflected by the companies' relatively low McDep ratios.

67

TABLE 4.1 U.S. OIL AND GAS INTEGRATED COMPANIES
MCDEP: (STOCK MARKET CAPITALIZATION AND DEBT)/PROPERTY
U.S. OIL AND GAS IN THE GROUND AT $12/BBL AND $1.50/MCF
RANKED BY MCDEP

	PRICE 10/19 1987 ($/SH)	SHARES (MM)	MARKET CAP ($MM)	DEBT ($MM)	MARKET CAP & DEBT ($MM)	PROP ($MM)	DEBT/ PROP	MCDEP RATIO	PV EQUITY ($/SH)	STOCK APPRECIATION POTENTIAL (%)
Small										
American Petrofina	64	13	840	400	1,240	1,350	.30	.92	73	14
Total (North America)	15	24	360	400	760	980	.41	.78	24	61
Pennzoil	51	48	2,500	1,700	4,200	6,000	.28	.70	90	75
Crown Central (low vote rights)	16	9	140	70	210	310	.23	.68	27	67
Quaker State	15	26	400	50	450	690	.07	.65	25	61
Murphy	29	34	1,000	600	1,600	2,500	.24	.64	57	95
Kerr-McGee	36	48	1,700	1,200	2,900	4,800	.25	.60	75	110
Phillips	12	230	2,700	8,500	11,200	18,800	.45	.60	45	280
Unocal	29	116	3,300	7,400	10,700	19,200	.39	.56	102	250
Amerada Hess	23	89	2,100	1,800	3,900	7,300	.25	.53	62	170
Sun	36	108	3,900	3,100	7,000	15,700	.20	.45	117	220
Composite			19,000	25,000	44,000	77,000	.32	.57		170
Large										
British Petroleum	60	460	27,700	20,000	47,700	58,000	.34	.82	83	37
Exxon	34	1,440	48,000	24,000	72,000	108,000	.22	.67	58	74
USX	22	270	5,800	10,000	15,800	25,000	.40	.63	56	160
Atlantic Richfield	65	180	11,700	15,000	26,700	43,000	.35	.62	156	140
Royal Dutch/Shell	95	450	43,000	19,000	62,000	100,000	.19	.62	180	90
Mobil	32	410	13,200	17,000	30,200	53,000	.32	.57	88	170
Texaco	33	270	8,800	9,000	17,800	34,000	.26	.52	93	180
Chevron	41	340	14,000	12,000	26,000	50,000	.24	.52	112	170
Amoco	60	260	15,600	11,000	26,600	53,000	.21	.50	162	170
Composite			188,000	137,000	325,000	524,000	.26	.62		106

One important reason is investor skepticism about management's success at reinvesting what can amount to billions of dollars of cash flow every year. Influenced by past performances in the oil business, investors are understandably fearful that a company's stock price may never reflect the actual value of its underlying properties because management is going to continue doing a poor job of reinvesting the cash flow from these properties—basically by pouring money into existing diversified operations and the refining/marketing business, a notoriously cyclical industry with low historical returns on capital investment. From this comes investor unwillingness to pay more in the stock market. Investors must trust management to reinvest the cash flow wisely and successfully, and that's generally a bigger leap of faith than they want to make.

Indeed, it is a rare oil company that can fare well not only as an integrated concern, but can also manage minerals and petrochemicals and retail stores in a profitable manner. When management insists on keeping these varied operations under one corporate roof, top managers are not only overextended—in my estimation—but forced to become "portfolio managers" as they allocate cash flow. Unfortunately, oil companies don't pay these managers high enough fees to justify spending the time necessary to invest wisely in such diverse areas. For instance, if the $30 billion present value of Amoco's equity were a pension fund or a mutual fund, the annual investment management fee might be one quarter of one percent, or more than $75 million. The top twenty executive officers of Amoco earned less than $6 million in 1986. No wonder that only a small proportion of Amoco's capital is efficiently invested and that the company's stock has languished in recent years.

Therefore, one of my themes has been, "Let investors invest and managers manage." By downsizing an integrated oil company and creating more concentrated entities, management can focus on the business it knows best— whether it be exploration and production or refining and marketing. Investors, meanwhile, can pick those areas of the energy business that appear most attractive.

The stocks of integrated oil companies are also weighed down by their image of being conglomerates. This means, for example, that since few investors can be thoroughly familiar with all functions of a diversified and integrated company, the strength of a particular part is not likely to be fully appreciated. Meanwhile, perceived weaknesses or adverse developments in another wing of the company can unduly restrain stock performance. So ultimately the stock price has trouble reflecting the total value of its respective pieces. Investors are usually overly fearful of the weaker link while too inclined to undervalue the potential strengths. Moreover, while a company that combines several functions will typically be valued on the performance that management can achieve from the total, that performance is often worse than what these pieces could achieve if they were able to function out on their own as independent entities. I know that as an investor myself, when I can analyze a pure play company (e.g., an independent oil and gas producer) and become familiar with all aspects of its operation, I'm much more willing to pay a higher relative stock price. But when that company is a USX, with a sizable investment in a depressed industry—steel—that I'm much less knowledgeable about, then I'm cautious about what I will pay for the stock.

Integrated stock prices can also reflect a tug-of-war between two different investment personalities. On the one side are investors oriented to the long term who favor the steadier and ultimately more lucrative earnings and cash flow trend provided by exploration and production (excepting a year like 1986, of course). On the opposing side are investors with a much shorter investment horizon who prefer the cyclical opportunities in refining and marketing. Neither camp is entirely comfortable with an investment that must include the other side of the oil business, and this uneasy coexistence harms the stock's potential.

RESTRUCTURING STEPS TO BRING OUT GREATER SHAREHOLDER VALUE

If I felt it was going to be "business as usual" at my targeted integrated oil companies, I would be much less enthused about their stock market prospects, except as a play on rising oil and gas prices. But investors, through McDep, are delivering a clear signal as to how these integrated companies can bring out far greater value for shareholders, and I'm confident that outside pressures—coupled with management changes and a bit more enlightenment—will hasten appropriate restructuring.

Basically, the stock market suggests rather strongly that these diversified, integrated oil companies should turn themselves into smaller, more efficient pieces that will be better regarded by investors. After all, companies like Unocal and Amoco have much lower McDep ratios than independent refiners, producers, and trusts and partnerships.

Here are four possible restructuring steps that the managements of integrated oil companies should consider taking, not only to achieve a much higher overall stock price, but to contribute to a more efficient oil industry. As an investor, you should look for this restructuring potential in the companies you follow and note whatever progress management is making. Ultimately, these steps will give a company greater stock market recognition and price appreciation potential.

1. REDUCE DIVERSIFICATION

Certain managements should complete the encouraging trend of recent years by divesting (selling) and spinning off their unrelated businesses such as minerals, retail stores, and even chemicals. Reducing diversification frees management's time, energy, and resources to concentrate on the company's oil and gas operations.

Some managements (notably at Tenneco and Kerr-McGee) argue that diversification provides higher assurance of an attractive long-term rate of return by providing a balance against volatile areas of the energy business. Yet we know from history that U.S. oil companies have been drained of billions of dollars by various diversification forays that have left little to show for all this investment.

Amoco set a good example in 1985 when it spun off Cyprus Minerals to shareholders on a 1-to-10 share basis (meaning ten shares of Cyprus for every one hundred shares of Amoco), acknowledging at the time that its original investment in minerals had been a bad decision. This move allowed Cyprus to stand alone, where its considerable virtues—even at a time of depressed commodity markets—could be recognized by investors and analyzed separate from the integrated structure. Investors looking for diversification into minerals didn't care about Cyprus when it was isolated deep within Amoco—a $1 billion minnow inside a $30 billion whale—but they liked its prospects as an independent entity and they could act on their convictions. Indeed, Cyprus stock rose from $12 to $24 in about a year's time and marched higher in 1987 on the growing strength of its gold, copper, and coal operations. Original Amoco shareholders who chose to retain their Cyprus stock thus found themselves with a promising long-term investment in the minerals business. (An even better example has been the success of Battle Mountain Gold, spun off from Pennzoil on a 1-to-1 share basis at $10—and rising as high as $45 in 1987.)

Chemicals represent a more controversial aspect of diversification. Although this sector is more closely related to oil and gas refining than minerals and has become the most important nonoil business for many companies, I still think spinoffs make more sense.

At Amoco, for example, chemicals clearly are helping the bottom line, and the bottom line helps the stock, but chemicals would be worth more as a separate company— to Amoco as well as its stockholders. Amoco's management *likes* the chemicals business, but few investors buy Amoco stock with chemicals in mind; if they cared that strongly about the business, they would buy an independent chemicals company. Companies like Amoco should actually be taking advantage of these profitable times for chemicals by selling or spinning off their operations into a strong market. Obviously that's what USX decided when it sold its chemical company, Aristech, as part of a restructuring program in 1986. (Atlantic Richfield made a similar move in 1987 by selling 20 percent of Arco Chemical Company to the public for $550 million, thereby establishing a stock market value of $2.2 billion on its remaining chemical operations.)

Some oil managers argue that another reason for holding on to their chemical operations is the fact that years of effort and millions of dollars have gone into acquiring proprietary technology and establishing market positions for their chemical products. My response is that these virtues can be far better appreciated when they are a recognizable, integral part of an independent company than when submerged inside a huge corporation.

2. USE SPINOFFS TO HIGHLIGHT PROPERTY VALUES

Managements of integrated oil companies should be enhancing shareholder value by spinning off exploration and production properties—either as limited partnerships or as independent companies, depending on the parent company's tax status. Although changes in the tax laws will discourage certain companies from creating a limited partnership, others will still find it advantageous. Over forty trusts and partnerships exist today, yet just three have been formed by integrated companies (Unocal, Diamond Shamrock, and Sun), leaving considerable potential within the group.

At Unocal, for example, the successful spinoff of Union Exploration Partners has helped investors recognize— and appreciate—the company's true underlying property values. Unocal created the partnership in May 1985 as part of its desperate effort to foil Mesa's takeover attempt. The company spun off about 30 percent of its total properties (primarily Gulf Coast oil and gas assets), but retained ownership of 95 percent of the partnership units (shares) and continued as the managing partner. So, in effect, Union Exploration Partners holds properties that are identical to 30 percent of the properties held by Unocal.

Here's where McDep helps reinforce my convictions about the long-term potential in Unocal stock. In mid-1987, Union Exploration Partners was selling for $19 a share, representing a stock market capitalization of $4.6 billion and a McDep ratio of 1.21. Yet all of Unocal, at $40 a share, had a market cap of just $4.6 billion and a McDep of .84. Obviously, all of Unocal's properties would be worth far more in the stock market if they were all spun off into appropriate partnerships or companies, leaving Unocal with its "downstream" operations (everything from the wellhead to the consumer). In fact, *all* of Unocal's oil and gas properties could be selling at a McDep of 1.21—the same as Union Exploration Partners—and thus support a stock price of well over $80 at today's going rate for oil and gas in the ground.

3. PURSUE 'DEINTEGRATION'

While the major oil companies embrace the diversification offered by refining and marketing, the stock market sends a clear signal that integration actually contributes to lower stock prices. Just look to McDep for evidence that investors assign greater relative value to the pieces of an integrated company than to the parent itself. Refining/marketing in particular is such a volatile, low-margin type of business that it connotes poor investment decisions by management and inefficient use of cash flow.

Companies should thus offset this penalty and shed the integrated image by separating refining and marketing from exploration and production. This can be accomplished by either selling the downstream operations (especially if the parent company needs cash and the market conditions are favorable), or better yet, spin them off to shareholders and let the stock market establish a value for this new entity. That means the value of the transaction isn't dependent on management's judgment as to what is the best price, and existing stockholders can decide for themselves whether they want to own a piece of this new company or sell and reinvest. If they still want to participate in refining/marketing, they can now invest in a pure play company.

A spinoff of refining/marketing also benefits existing stockholders by giving them equal amounts of shares in this new company and the surviving production company. When the two pieces establish their own value in the stock market, their combined value should easily exceed the stock price of the original company at the time of the announced spinoff.

Still, my deintegration proposals receive spirited opposition from oil industry leaders. In 1986, an aberrational boom year for refining/marketing as oil prices took their epic plunge, the common remark was, "Gee, we're glad we have refining and marketing. Where would we be without them?" Indeed, soaring downstream profits helped most integrated companies post surprisingly good earnings and sustain their dividend payments. But realistically, those companies not saddled with excessive debt would have survived the year without refining/marketing profits, and by year's end would have been reflecting even greater stock market enthusiasm as oil prices continued to strengthen. Most integrated companies did enjoy a good rally in early 1987, but they were also being penalized by predictions that downstream profits would be sharply lower in 1987.

Looking back on 1986, let's presume that Mobil had deintegrated the year before by turning all of its exploration/production operations into partnerships, while retaining a Mobil USA refining/marketing company. Obviously the remaining Mobil piece would have enjoyed a strong runup in stock value, judging by the performance of other refiners and marketers such as Ashland, Total, Quaker State, and Getty Petroleum. Meanwhile, Mobil's production pieces would have eroded a bit in the spring and summer before recovering late in the year; even in a lousy year like 1986, independent production companies still retained high McDep ratios, along with most partnerships. The Mobil production pieces would have had sufficient cash flow to maintain a good dividend, while Mobil refining and marketing profits might have justified an even higher payout.

In a December 1986 report, my colleague Phil Dodge warned his readers not to forget production. "The danger from the great downstream results in 1986 is that investors may start watching the wrong ball," he said. "In fact, oil and gas reserves have almost always been the tap root of values for oil companies because of the discovery element that can instantly create wealth and the sizable amount of cash generation during production." He added, "The reputation of crude oil as a pillar of worth has been badly tarnished in 1986 by the crash in prices. However, prices for oil production now appear to be on the mend at the same time that refining/marketing margins are returning to the narrow range that is a more normal condition." (He was quite prescient with these observations.)

Originally, when the United States had a surplus of crude oil production, it made some sense for oil companies to expand downstream into refining and marketing. John D. Rockefeller's original argument, for example, was that he wanted to insure an outlet for more of his crude oil by controlling the market from exploration down to the gas pump. Another spur for integration occurred about 1933 when companies needed to find more markets for East Texas oil that was selling for 15¢ a barrel.

Today, however, the United States is a net importer of oil, which means that domestic producers can sell every barrel of oil they produce (with the exception of some heavy crude oil in California), without having to own refineries. Rarely are there strategic advantages to being integrated these days. The Amerada Hess refinery in New Jersey, for instance, doesn't process any of Amerada's crude oil production from North Dakota. Since the business arguments for integration are also weak at best, the only remaining justification for remaining integrated may be no more than, "We have always been in refining," or "We're going to be just like Exxon."

A common argument against my deintegration theme is the fear that many newly independent refining/marketing companies might not survive outside the integrated structure. But if that's the case, why should an existing integrated company support such an inherently weak operation? If such a company cannot survive (given a reasonable amount of help by the parent company at the time of the spinoff), why should it be subsidized in disguised form? An efficient, well-run refiner will survive out on its own, and those entities that can't survive won't be missed—especially if the oil industry is to avoid becoming another steel industry. In fact, I've long argued that deintegration would improve the entire oil industry by forcing refining/marketing operations to become more efficient, while freeing exploration and production units from having to support their poorer relations in most years. One example would be the fact that an independent refining company must go to investors and lenders to raise money to build a major new facility. Earlier this decade, some unwise expansion projects by a number of integrated companies might not have been launched under that discipline. Yet the money is available to smaller entities with worthwhile plans.

My skeptics also worry about deintegration's effect on the "upstream" (exploration and production) side of business, particularly in terms of this country's strategic positioning in the world. They argue, for example, that the United States needs giant integrated oil companies in order

78

to compete internationally, that only these companies with deep financial pockets can afford to explore the frontiers for vital future supplies of oil. In reality, however, corporate size is not the crucial factor it might appear to be. Thanks to sophisticated risk-sharing mechanisms, where companies take percentages of each other's projects, a $1 billion or $2 billion exploration company can participate anywhere in the world, buying leases and sinking exploratory wells. As a result, a company as small as Murphy Oil, with just $1.7 billion in property value, can participate in some of the most expensive "hot" prospects. The magnet for putting money into an exploration project is the quality of the program; if the venture is promising, we can raise money right on Wall Street through public offerings of a company's stock and special drilling programs (though I personally prefer to invest my money in the stock market). Moreover, the characteristics of U.S. exploration today call for a better match of size of company with size of prospects. New discoveries of oil and gas fields are smaller and smaller, and since a new discovery is more important to a smaller organization than to a larger one, it gets more careful attention.

Overall, I'll agree that integration provides certain operating benefits, but not to the extent that we need nearly twenty integrated oil companies. The operating benefits that do exist can be preserved by contractual arrangements between the new refining company and the residual production company when deintegration occurs. And threats of a classic "squeeze" of one function against another do not appear very menacing as long as most of the industry remains integrated. If anything, the federal government tends to protect independents, whether they be refiners, marketers, explorers, or producers.

Ultimately, the stock market disadvantages that come

with integration override any operational benefits, and managements that continue to insist on preserving this combination of functions are doing their stockholders a disservice. Yet here's the kind of response you can expect to hear from the typical supporter of integration: If the refining/marketing environment is weak, the argument will be that newly created refining/marketing companies can't survive on their own; but if the outlook is promising (meaning that oil prices are declining), then oil companies should hang on to refining to bolster the bottom line. My answer is always, "Whether times are good or bad, the combined value of the separate pieces would be worth more than the original integrated company."

Former Texaco chairman John McKinley argued in 1986 that refiners and producers "have to hang together" in an increasingly competitive world. My point would be that they can compete quite effectively on their own, but together they are doomed to mediocrity.

4. KEEP THE RESTRUCTURED PIECES RELATIVELY SMALL

Since many stock market investors view size itself as a negative, oil managers should look for ways to reduce the size of the pure pieces that might remain particularly large after deintegration.

For example, splitting Texaco into just two pieces would still leave two giant companies—a $5 billion refining/marketing operation and a $19 billion exploration and production company. At that size, neither piece would likely command a McDep ratio higher than 1.0. By comparison, the leading independent refiner, Ashland Oil, is about a $3 billion company, while the largest independent production company, Maxus Energy (formerly Diamond Shamrock), has just $3 billion in property value.

So I've recommended turning Texaco into perhaps eight independent pieces by subdividing its operations along functional and geographical lines, in each of those functional areas. These new entities, trading in the stock market, could still average about $3 billion in property value—certainly large enough to succeed on their own. Remember, even a $2 billion company can explore for oil along with the big boys, so the creation of numerous exploration companies from one large piece is not going to undermine United States exploration efforts. In fact, exploration efforts in the United States and Canada are often promoted by small companies who raise money from other companies for an exploration project. On the production side, even during a disastrous year like 1986 there were still healthy independent companies with McDep ratios of 1.0 or more. Their earnings were depressed but they were still producing cash flow from their properties.

How would Texaco shareholders benefit from the kind of restructuring I've outlined? Well, if we started with the original piece of Texaco at $33 (representing a McDep ratio of just .66) and we created eight separate entities that traded for a composite McDep of 1.0, the actual stock value would be $63 today—and $93 down the road, assuming $1 billion is eventually paid to Pennzoil to settle their suit. That's a lot of value to be brought out at Texaco. Similar downsizing potential exists at my other targeted integrated companies, as we'll see.

ISOLATING THE 'BEST' LOW-MCDEP COMPANIES

Well into the next decade, shareholders should be profiting from the streamlining of the U.S. oil industry as integrated companies are restructured, either by existing managements or following a takeover. This represents a less widespread trend than the sheer impact of continually higher energy prices, but you should move now to position yourself in several promising candidates so that you reap the stock market profits that result when restructuring plans are announced and eventually implemented.

The trick, of course, is to identify an integrated company that will indeed yield this bonus payoff. This leads us on a search for "vulnerable value."

My McDep technique guides us to the integrated group and isolates the most undervalued companies at any given time—in an objective, statistical fashion. But my subsequent enthusiasm for a particular low-McDep company also reflects further research and certain subjective factors that emerge as I look into the company and try to substantiate the "buy" signal issued by McDep. I prefer to bet on a low-McDep company in which I can perceive that management is either vulnerable to an outright takeover bid, under pressure from major shareholders to make structural changes, or at least seemingly open to restructuring ideas. Here are some of the signs that I look for and evaluate as I do my homework:

1. *What is the company's past stock performance?* Since McDep analysis looks to the future, I normally downplay a company's past performance in the stock market (as measured by total return: stock price appreciation plus dividends). Occasionally, however, a company's historical record can indicate that management is particularly vulnerable to shareholder pressures for change and that it may lack necessary investor support in the event of a proxy challenge or tender offer.

Using total return as a gauge for past management performance, Table 4.2 lists the fifteen-year records for integrated oil companies, starting in mid–1971 when I joined Donaldson, Lufkin and Jenrette. I also list the relative performance of these companies from 1981 to 1986. Notice how one of my targeted companies, Amerada Hess, easily stands out at the bottom of the small integrated group, whether your concern is long-term or short-term performance. Investors have earned such a scant return for so many years that existing management would have a difficult time mustering support against a rival set of directors, nominated by any disgruntled shareholder who was willing to expend the necessary time, effort, and expense. Texaco, with the poorest record among the large integrated companies, was only marginally more successful than Amerada Hess. In fact, if it hadn't been for the company's strong dividend, investors wouldn't have made any money at all on the stock over that fifteen-year period.

As long as management remains entrenched at Amerada Hess and Texaco, shareholders may have to suffer "business as usual," but I'm optimistic that such poor historical records eventually will bring about changes that contribute to sharply higher stock prices. If given the chance, restless shareholders—certainly with no deep-seated loyalty to management—would

TABLE 4.2 TOTAL RETURN TO STOCKHOLDERS
(STOCK PRICE CHANGE, PLUS DIVIDENDS AND OTHER DISTRIBUTIONS)

(1971–86)
(PERCENT PER YEAR)

SMALL INTEGRATED COMPANIES		LARGE INTEGRATED COMPANIES	
Pennzoil	15	Royal Dutch	16
Unocal	12	Exxon	16
Phillips	11	Amoco	15
Sun	10	British Petroleum	13
USX	5	Chevron	12
Kerr-McGee	3	Mobil	12
Amerada Hess	1	Atlantic Richfield	11
		Texaco	7

(1981–86)

Sun	13	Royal Dutch	27
Pennzoil	13	Exxon	22
Phillips	7	British Petroleum	15
Unocal	4	Mobil	9
Kerr-McGee	–3	Amoco	7
USX	–6	Atlantic Richfield	6
Amerada Hess	–7	Chevron	6
		Texaco	6

very likely vote for opposition directors, and neither management could seriously defend its past performance.

2. *Has management taken unpopular actions?* Certain decisions by management may weaken a company's stock performance and chip away at shareholder loyalty, thus increasing the likelihood of outside pressure on management to improve performance—or risk a takeover.

A good example would be USX, which made an ill-advised, poorly timed buyout of Texas Oil and Gas in November 1985, diluting the holdings of existing shareholders and expanding the company's energy presence at a time when the near-term outlook for oil pricing was tenuous at best. As the stock sagged from $26 toward $14 in 1986 (helped along, of course, by plunging oil prices and steel's continuing slump) and shareholder resentment increased, USX management felt compelled to begin restructuring the company. The process was hastened along by Carl Icahn's $31-a-share tender offer (eventually withdrawn), which helped the stock surpass my estimated breakup value of $37 a share in mid-1987.

Another example here would be beleaguered Texaco, where management gave the term "greenmail" real meaning in 1984 by paying $1.2 billion to the Bass Brothers to forestall a potential takeover bid. Texaco paid $52 a share for the Bass holdings, well above the going market price in the high $30s. Management then proceeded to bungle its defense against the Pennzoil lawsuit (which arose out of Texaco's takeover of Getty), eventually resulting in a $10 billion judgment against Texaco and depressing the stock's performance all through 1986 and most of 1987.

3. *Are there any overt signs that disenchanted stockholders are pressuring management for specific actions?* Business stories in newspapers or magazines may tip you off that management is under fire from major stockholders (or influential analysts!). Another signal would be shareholder resolutions in the company's annual proxy statement that call for specific restructuring steps or try to make management more accountable to shareholders and less entrenched against a takeover bid. While these resolutions may not generate sufficient votes to pass, they serve a useful function by focusing attention on how management can take action to help improve the company's stock performance.

4. *Does management appear receptive to potential restructuring efforts?* I'm always looking for signs indicating management's relative willingness—or stubbornness—about making important restructuring moves, particularly in terms of deintegration and divesting nonenergy operations. At Unocal, for example, Chairman Fred Hartley has been so vociferously opposed to my constructive suggestions over the years that Unocal management is obviously unwilling to do any meaningful restructuring while Mr. Hartley remains in charge. I've experienced the same type of rigid opposition at Amerada Hess, where Leon Hess rules virtually unchallenged. But I'm still recommending both companies for other reasons, as you'll see. And I do have higher hopes for management-inspired changes at other low-McDep

targets such as Amoco and Mobil, who have shown a willingness to seek out greater value for shareholders in recent years.

5. *What is the takeover potential?* Even though takeovers have made a number of my recommendations successful in the past, I do not recommend buying stocks simply because they are takeover candidates. Takeovers obviously bring a quicker, more dramatic payoff on your investment, but that's a risky, Las Vegas way to play the game. My preference is to have existing management voluntarily make the changes I'm talking about that will make money for you. A voluntary, ongoing restructuring program (as we've seen in Atlantic Richfield and Exxon in recent years) can prove equally and perhaps even more rewarding over a longer time frame and is a more realistic prospect.

Still, I certainly look at how enticing a low-McDep company might be to an outside bidder. I try to sense how realistic any takeover effort might be, given the size of the target company, how much of the stock is held by management and other insiders, and the appeal of the company's various assets—particularly its concentration on U.S. oil and gas reserves. The company's low McDep has already spotlighted the value disparity between stock price and properties, indicating management's potential vulnerability.

Although the frenzied takeover era of 1981–85 has given way to a different environment today, key catalysts such as Boone Pickens, Carl Icahn, and Australia's Robert Holmes à Court are still in the hunt, and six major integrated companies are smaller than the largest previous takeover "victim," Gulf

Oil. Using estimated property value as my basis of comparison, Kerr-McGee, Pennzoil, Amerada Hess, Sun Oil, Phillips, and Unocal are all smaller than the ultimate Gulf deal (a $17 billion transaction, including $13 billion in market cap paid by Chevron and $4 billion in Gulf debt).

So the tender offer by an outside investor or corporation remains a powerful potential technique for changing corporate control in the oil industry. Even a failed takeover bid (as we've seen at USX and Diamond Shamrock) can exert the necessary pressure on management to restructure.

6. *What is management's potential accountability to shareholders?* While the seven or eight largest integrated companies may prove impervious to an actual takeover attempt, the growing success of the shareholder revolution should at least contribute "watchdog" pressure on most of these managements. As shareholders become increasingly organized and determined to bring about important changes at their companies—especially by championing meaningful proxy resolutions and nominating opposition directors—then even the most entrenched managements at the largest companies could begin to feel the heat. We might even go after Exxon one day, though the company has certainly made many of the right moves in recent years to enhance shareholder value (e.g., by selling off nonenergy assets and maintaining an aggressive stock purchase program).

CURRENT 'ACTION'
RECOMMENDATIONS

Taking into account the specific factors emphasized in this chapter, I would focus on the following companies: Amerada Hess, Amoco, Chevron, Kerr-McGee, Mobil, Phillips, Texaco, and Unocal. The restructuring trend may be silent as you read this book, muted by rising stock prices in 1987, but it can recur at any moment, especially if certain stocks weaken a bit and no longer look as overpriced to a value hunter like Boone Pickens. Meanwhile, continuing takeovers and restructurings in the nonenergy sector serve to highlight my favorite low-McDep companies as having significant ''vulnerable value'' that can be brought out in the stock market.

Since there's no guarantee of appropriate management actions at any of my recommended companies—only the strong likelihood that various pressures will compel management to act on behalf of shareholders—you should try to have several of these stocks in your portfolio at any given time. By spreading your bets, all of your integrated stocks stand to benefit when a takeover attempt or announced restructuring at one company fans investor excitement for the group as a whole.

Of course, my recommended stocks also represent compelling commodity plays in the strengthening energy business. By investing in these low-McDep stocks now, you not only stand to reap the benefits of restructuring, but can win on commodity leverage as oil and gas prices keep moving higher.

In the company profiles that follow, remember that my rationales for a particular stock are based on what I knew at the time. Given the nature of the energy business today, make sure you do a little homework on any company you buy stock in so that you're aware of any important developments that could affect a stock's relative appeal—and payoff potential. (In Chapter 7 I'll show you how to update a company's McDep ratio and how to use the McDep technique and other tactics as you buy, hold, and sell your integrated stocks over the years.)

If the price of a particular stock is lower than what I've listed here, that should represent an opportunity to start building a position at an attractive price. Conversely, if a stock has run to the upside and now sports a notably higher McDep ratio, you should postpone any purchase and instead simply focus on the stocks that are still lagging the group in terms of their McDep ratios.

AMOCO

Stock price, 10/19/87: $68
McDep ratio: .62
Yield: 5.5 percent

This has been my laggard blue-chip recommendation in recent years, a stock that has grown increasingly compelling in my McDep tables. Now, with formidable long-life oil and gas reserves, coupled with impeccable corporate finances, Amoco offers exciting participation in a rebounding industry. Compared to its high-quality rivals, Exxon and Royal Dutch (who performed spectacularly in 1986 and most of 1987), Amoco has a greater concentration on U.S. oil and gas production, and as prices for these resources continue to rise, Amoco stock should reflect the escalating value of its underlying reserves.

Equally important from an investment standpoint, Amoco's low McDep ratio—poorest among the large integrated companies—highlights tremendous potential for restructuring. The company's size and relatively strong historical performance (a total return of 15 percent from 1971 to 1986) buffers management from a takeover attempt or shareholder unrest. But they could certainly be more aggressive and innovative in undertaking programs to realize the full value of Amoco's vast properties. The company's present value of equity is $104 in my $8/$1.10 tables and $162 with $12/$1.50 values for oil and gas in the ground.

Amoco management showed promise in 1985 by spinning off Cyprus Minerals and launching a stock buyback program, but that program was halted too early, while other restructuring moves have yet to occur. So here are some of the steps I think Amoco should take to bring out more immediate value for shareholders, while also signaling to investors that management is indeed concerned about realizing the company's historical promise.

1. Increase the dividend (which could be comfortably supported by cash flow).
2. Relaunch a $4 billion to $5 billion stock buyback program. Taking on debt to carry out this program would be easy for a company that has a debt-to-property ratio of just .21.
3. Spin off the well-regarded chemical operations (second largest among the oil companies) to existing Amoco shareholders. This independent unit would rank impressively in size with Monsanto and Dow Chemical and could command perhaps $20 a share, given today's improved climate for chemical companies. Although Amoco is pleased with its chemical unit, the operation is buried inside the integrated structure and provides little help for Amoco stock.

4. Spin off U.S. refining and marketing into an estimated $4 billion entity that might trade for more than $10 a share in today's market.

5. Create several independent exploration and production pieces in the United States, Canada, and overseas that Amoco stockholders could retain—or sell—at their own discretion. Amoco has long been the leading explorer in the United States, and its existing exploration company probably could command a top price in the stock market because investors could support a long-term commitment by top people, based on their reputation and past exploration success. Meanwhile, Amoco's existing oil reserves (with a reserve-life index of eleven years) would provide a solid underpinning for any newly formed production company. Overall, Amoco has unusually high-quality characteristics in U.S. exploration and production that warrant special attention, whether they remain part of Amoco's $38 billion empire or are reflected in a new operation.

6. Owning about 20 percent of the Hugoton gas reserves in Kansas, Amoco could place these prized holdings into a new corporation. That would still leave the company strongly positioned in natural gas, since it already has the most reserves of any integrated oil company. This includes vast holdings in the overlooked Overthrust belt of Colorado and Wyoming. These reserves are not yet economical, but with gas coming back, companies like Amoco and Chevron—who have the lion's share of Overthrust reserves—eventually should profit quite nicely.

WILL MANAGEMENT ACT?

Although Amoco's fifteen-year record into 1986 was among the best of all the oil companies, the company's stock performance has been steadily fading in recent years relative to the large integrated group. Most of Amoco's long-term investors seem to be satisfied with the company's performance, but I feel their opinion of management quality is unduly high. Decent people run the company, but they're too conservative; instead of using Amoco's impressive financial resources to achieve more value, they simply hoard capital and nurture their Triple A credit rating. The company's low-McDep ratio signifies that management is certainly not doing its job on behalf of shareholders.

In addition to pruning Amoco through sales and spin-offs, management should use its financial strength to gain control of a weaker low-McDep company and reward the shareholders of both companies. Using borrowed money, Amoco could gain control of an Amerada Hess or Texaco, then pay down its debt by selling off unrelated assets, while holding on to valuable oil and gas reserves. (Amoco took a major step in this direction by bidding $3.86 billion for Dome Petroleum of Canada in mid-1987.)

I first recommended Amoco in May 1979 at $32, and the stock eventually rose to $99½ in late 1980 before splitting 2-for-1. After removing the stock from my recommended list in June 1982, I reiterated my recommendation in August 1985, when it stood at $63½. Now I'm waiting patiently for the enormous value I see in Amoco to come out—eventually. Royal Dutch, an equally high-quality, low-debt company, was a low-McDep outfit in early 1986 and it eventually doubled within a year. I'm looking for a similar payoff in Amoco, though not necessarily over such a short time frame.

AMERADA HESS

Stock price, 10/19/87: $23
McDep ratio: .68
Yield: 1.3 percent

In May 1986 I appeared at the annual meeting of Amerada Hess stockholders in Woodbridge, New Jersey, to present my shareholder proposal to divide the company into three publicly traded pieces: one for refining/marketing operations, two for exploration and production. Speaking to about four hundred people, I noted that I represented my wife, Louise, who had offered the proposal. "Louise and I live in New Jersey and I am a petroleum investment analyst by profession," I said. "You might wonder about my judgment as an investment analyst because we own Amerada Hess stock. Don't blame Louise for that. Every time we buy more shares she groans, 'We never make any money on that stock.' "

We certainly weren't alone. Amerada Hess stock was trading for $22 a share—exactly what it was fifteen years earlier, when I started working on Wall Street. Over that span it had the poorest record of any major oil company, returning just 1 percent a year in stock market appreciation and dividends. Total return actually *declined* 7 percent from 1981 to 1986. While it was true that Amerada had offered good trading opportunities over the years, rising sharply on periodic takeover speculation and swings in the volatile refining and marketing business, the stock invariably retreated to the low $20s.

This indefensible record, compiled by a management that had become increasingly entrenched and ineffective, obscured the company's valuable oil and gas properties and convinced me that it was time for shareholders to revolt. I appreciated Amerada's investment potential, but I

94

knew nothing was going to happen unless management felt the pressure to make changes that would bring out the value of those properties.

My 1986 resolution to recreate Amerada Hess as three separate companies, and a similar proposal in 1987, both attracted about 9 percent of the vote. This mini-revolution certainly failed to topple management, but I do think we prodded them into action. At the 1987 annual meeting, management declared its intention to reinstate the dividend it suspended a year earlier, to repurchase stock, and to announce other value-enhancing moves in the near future. In the face of that good news, I started deemphasizing Amerada's stock as a new commitment.

"While the potential for appreciation remains attractive," I wrote (when the stock was about $37), "stock repurchase will increase the percentage of ownership of the major shareholder, who has been responsible for the company's unsatisfactory historic performance. So although this buyback program has a positive near-term effect, it doesn't solve the long-term problem."

The obvious key to developments at Amerada lies in what Leon Hess ultimately decides to do as the company's autocratic chairman and major shareholder (with 17 percent of the stock outstanding). He's 73 and seemingly near retirement, but Armand Hammer, at 89, is still running Occidental Petroleum. While Mr. Hess may indeed retire— his health in recent years has not been good—he might also try to turn the company over to his son, John, who has a high-level position but unproven abilities. That might suit Mr. Hess, but certainly not most stockholders, and it could precipitate a hostile takeover effort.

Financially, the company is obviously susceptible to a takeover, with only $7.3 billion in property value. Management has tried to forestall that fate with super-majority rule, which requires an 80 percent vote to approve any major transaction *opposed* by the board of directors. Since Mr. Hess owns some 17 percent of the stock, it will be nearly impossible to achieve such a super majority. Nevertheless, management cannot turn down a reasonable offer lightly. To do so would generate intense opposition from disenchanted shareholders.

Of course, Mr. Hess could take actions on his own to transform his company, but he's a stubborn man and he admits that he can't bring himself to break up a company he has assembled over many years.

What's the potential value at Amerada Hess? The present breakup value is only $43 (but $62 under $12/$1.50 conditions), which Mr. Hess could more than achieve by creating three pieces: (1) a refining/marketing company, (2) an international exploration and production company, and (3) a U.S. exploration and production company.

Out on their own, the company's producing operations alone might sell at a combined $40 a share, even after absorbing a substantial portion of outstanding debt. The talented people already in this organization would control their own operations and make their own decisions, freed from an autocratic chairman who has always insisted on calling the shots while discouraging creative, independent thinking within his management.

Meanwhile, given the Hess brand name and a reasonably favorable industry outlook, the refining/marketing company could certainly command value in the stock market. Although the refining business has sharp ups and downs, growing U.S. dependence on imported oil will sustain demand for Amerada Hess's facilities, which thrived during the import boom of the 1960s and early 1970s. Current operations generate good cash flow and the new company would have additional value in its real estate holdings and oil inventories.

WHAT IS THE INVESTMENT RISK?

The main risk to owners of Amerada Hess is that Leon Hess will retain control and the company will be managed as unsuccessfully in the future as it has been in the past. Yet even without restructuring changes, the values remain attractive and the trends are favorable, greatly easing the potential risks as you wait for this stock to pay off. Here are some points to keep in mind:

- Earnings, particularly as reported by Amerada Hess, are an unreliable guide for measuring the company's ongoing progress. AHC's unusual use of FIFO accounting (whereby it treats inventories by the first-in, first-out method) leads to a mismatch of reported earnings and cash flow on an ongoing basis. This accounting quirk exacerbated the negative effect of lower oil prices on company earnings in 1986 and thereby contributed unfairly to stock market weakness by making the financial situation look worse than it really was.
- Cash flow before interest is a far more accurate indication of Amerada's financial strength. I've estimated this at $700 million in 1987, leaving plenty of room for the company to fully restore the dividend and increase the stock buyback program (though the latter, as I noted, is a mixed blessing by increasing management's ownership position).
- Despite the fact that many investors think of Amerada Hess as a weak refining/marketing company, explora-

tion and production are the dominant part of its actual property value. I've estimated that all of Amerada's crude-oil and natural gas properties have a value of $45 a share, of which approximately two-thirds are in the United States. This includes some high-quality properties with considerable untapped value. The company's concentrated representation in the North Sea would make an attractive acquisition for a company that wanted to expand exploration off Norway and didn't have existing production. Norwegian tax laws favor spending by existing producers.

As you assess and monitor all these conflicting issues at Amerada Hess, you may read the common defense raised by management, that their long-term commitment to shareholders is undermined by analysts such as myself who keep promoting "short-term" measures that have only one purpose—a higher stock price. Well, management accountability is the major issue here, and I would argue that fifteen years is enough time for management to prove itself. Clearly, after a total return of just 1 percent a year from 1971 to 1986, Amerada Hess deserves to be changed on behalf of long-suffering stockholders.

CHEVRON

Stock price, 10/19/87: $41
McDep ratio: .69
Yield: 5.8 percent

When I was nearing graduation from the University of Wisconsin about 25 years ago, George Keller came to campus to recruit me as a chemical engineer at Chevron. He went on to become today's chairman of that company while I went astray, to the point of actively campaigning for the deintegration and downsizing of integrated oil companies.

Yet despite my biases, I'm not about to steer you away from a blue-chip stock like Chevron that ought to be in your portfolio, especially if you can buy it when it looks good in the McDep rankings at current prices. Projecting toward 1990, when oil and gas could again approach their historic highs, Chevron's present value of equity is $112. So even though the stock has moved up from the mid-$30s since 1986, there's considerable long-term value still remaining within the McDep context.

The magic ingredient in Chevron's future potential is EOR—enhanced oil recovery—centered on its extensive heavy oil reserves in the Kern River field of California. George Keller even refers to Chevron as the "EOR company," citing a strategy to invest in this area of production on the basis that as oil prices march higher and conventional oil sources decline, EOR oil will become an increasingly valuable—and available—alternative to OPEC oil. Mr. Keller may be overstating the importance of enhanced oil recovery, but I know it represents a key to Chevron's ultimate stock appeal.

At first glance, heavy oil's appeal is obscured by the fact that it is more expensive to produce than conventional oil, since steam must be pumped into the ground through special injection wells in order to force the sludge-like crude oil to the surface. This steam is generated by burning oil or natural gas, with the ratio tending to be a barrel of fuel burned for every two barrels of oil brought up.

Not surprisingly, heavy oil production is not economical in most parts of the world today, but Kern County oil is a notable exception. Quite a bit is economical at $18 to $20 prices, and as these prices move higher, millions of barrels of additional output will be feasible—all from previously discovered fields.

The exciting feature about California's heavy-oil fields is that they offer a producer like Chevron double leverage of sorts as oil prices keep rising. First, the profit per barrel goes up—for heavy and conventional oil alike. But second, the number of recoverable barrels in an existing heavy-oil field goes up as more of the reserves become economical. Thus the reserve base expands and the producer can pump more barrels that earn a profit at higher prices. Bottom line: The profit margin improves disproportionately for each barrel of heavy oil relative to conventional oil.

As an investor, buying a company with significant heavy oil reserves means that the value of these reserves will rise more dramatically than the company's conventional oil reserves in a bullish energy environment. When you buy the stock, you pay the same price for each barrel of reserves, but as oil prices increase, so does the amount of EOR reserves that can now be produced. So not only are existing, already producing EOR reserves worth more, these reserves expand without any necessary exploration efforts. As a result, the overall gain in reserve value will be greater—percentagewise—for EOR oil than for conventional oil. For example, about 40 percent of Chevron's reported U.S. oil reserves might be heavy oil, but as oil prices go up, that 40 percent could double as increasing amounts of reserves become economic to produce. The 60 percent reported reserves of conventional oil wouldn't improve as much with higher prices, so Chevron's reserve base could move to 50 percent EOR and 50 percent conventional. Moreover, Chevron has traditionally been very conservative in reporting its heavy-oil reserves; this could mean positive surprises down the road as millions of barrels become available to replace production. (Other companies with EOR potential are basically those with established reserves in California: Unocal; Texaco, through its Getty acquisition; and Shell, a division of Royal Dutch.)

Ultimately, Chevron offers investors a significant concentration on U.S. oil reserves, thanks largely to its 1984 acquisition of Gulf Oil, which doubled proven domestic reserves and lessened the company's previous reliance on oil produced outside the United States. Domestic oil reserves now account for 34 percent of Chevron's property value, the fourth highest percentage among all the integrated companies—trailing only Atlantic Richfield (44 percent), Texaco (42 percent), and Sun (41 percent). On the exploration front, Chevron and British Petroleum are the only companies with subsurface drilling information from a test site near the Arctic National Wildlife Preserve in northern Alaska, which as I noted earlier is regarded as the only onshore area left in Alaska with the potential of another Prudhoe Bay. The two companies shared a testing well and have yet to release information on their findings.

Another fundamental reason I favor an investment in Chevron is the expert way management has absorbed Gulf Oil since paying $13.2 billion for that company in 1984, the largest corporate merger in history. Chevron has cut about 30,000 jobs from the merged operations and has sold off hunks of its refining and marketing business plus other low-return assets to bring its debt-to-property ratio under 30 percent. Meanwhile, it has retained most of Gulf's U.S. oil-producing properties and has resisted becoming overly diversified. The company is still too large, in my estimation, and could spin off certain assets into separate companies that would help improve Chevron's stock value.

On a financial basis, Chevron will generate about $4 billion to $4½ billion in cash flow in 1987, or about $1 billion more than capitalized outlays plus dividends. There could be a growing cushion here for a dividend hike or possibly a stock buyback program.

KERR-McGEE

Stock price, 10/19/87: $36
McDep ratio: .77
Yield: 3.1 percent

This Oklahoma-based company typifies how most of my low-McDep integrated companies eventually have their day as stock market performers.

In early February 1987, Kerr-McGee ($32 at the time) had fallen to the bottom of the pack with a .75 McDep ratio. Six months later it had improved in price to $39 and a McDep of .83, but still lagged behind every other company except Amoco and Texaco. I wrote at the time that the company "looks like a good commitment, but you may need a bit of patience to realize a major payoff because management has shown little initiative in maximizing values."

As it turned out, investors only needed conviction about McDep as a leading "buy" indicator, for in mid-August the company announced a major oil discovery in the North Sea and Kerr-McGee stock leaped over four points in two days to reach about $47, at a time when most energy stocks were under selling pressure.

Depending upon Kerr-McGee's stock price and relative McDep ratio today, you may want to delay any purchases, but it should still be an intriguing stock to monitor, for a number of reasons. For example:

256-3652

477-5092

Gumbo   Gocha
        RR2 Bof 20434
        Helablak

736-4344 Surssen
          124 W Enterprm
          blu Zyen

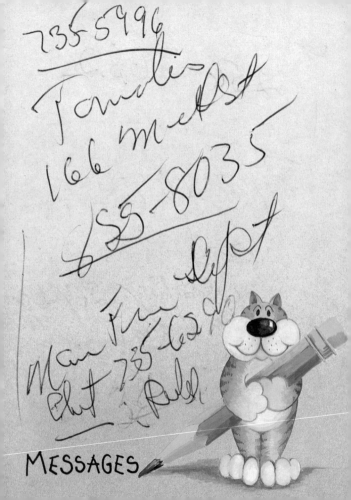

- *There's considerable restructuring potential at this energy conglomerate.* A third of the company's property value is represented by U.S. oil and gas reserves (a lower percentage than I prefer) and the remaining businesses include North Sea oil and gas, as well as coal, chemicals, contract drilling, refining/marketing, and uranium. The disadvantage of that diversity is that it's hard for any single investor to understand each business and to appreciate whatever distinctive strengths it might offer to Kerr-McGee. The advantage is that the company's overall stock market value can be greatly improved by appropriate spinoffs and divestitures.
- *The company could be subject to a hostile takeover bid, as rumored periodically since 1981.* Even with a "poison pill" defense in place, Kerr-McGee is an easily digestible target ($3.5 billion in property value plus $1 billion debt), and insiders hold only about 8 percent of the stock. Moreover, shareholder loyalty is tenuous at best, given the company's poor historical record since the early 1970s.
- *Strong ongoing cash flow and a debt-to-property ratio of only .29 should encourage management to resume a stock buyback program that was suspended in 1986.* The initial program to repurchase 20 percent of the company's stock stopped less than halfway there.

One underlying negative in Kerr-McGee's property value is the fact that its oil and gas holdings have reserve-life indexes of just five years and nine years respectively, both lower than industry averages. While the company presently generates impressive cash flow (still the best indicator of future value), these short-life reserves ultimately could cause a decline in the company's overall value. There's more risk realizing the potential value of properties if management does a poor job of reinvesting cash flow to replace declining reserves, since short-life reserves are produced faster than long-life reserves.

MOBIL

Stock price, 10/19/87: $32
McDep ratio: .74
Yield: 6.8 percent

I've had a strong interest in Mobil since July 1985, when I singled it out as my favorite candidate in the large integrated group, citing value and vulnerability as my criteria. Mobil (then $30 a share) had been plodding along for years, trading in a relatively narrow range as the stock market doubled and relying on its strong dividend and undervalued assets to keep investors interested. I knew, however, that most investors didn't have the necessary patience to wait out the eventual payoff I felt would ultimately result at Mobil. So I warned my clients, "The only real risk in Mobil is dullness." Boredom triggers impatience on Wall Street, often causing people to sell an undervalued stock too early, especially if a sudden upward pop in price gives them a 5- or 6-point profit.

Indeed, Mobil's stock was still mired at around $30 a year later. Although Mobil's new management, as promised, had been selling off nonpetroleum holdings to pay down debt, skeptics were unconvinced that chairman Allen Murray was indeed determined to bring out greater shareholder value—specifically, by jettisoning the survivors of its ill-fated Marcor acquisition in 1974, Container Corporation and Montgomery Ward. Yet that breakthrough came in late July 1986, when Mobil announced the sale of

Container Corporation, a paperboard packager, for $1.2 billion. Curiously, Mobil stock actually declined to below $30 in the next two days of trading, perhaps reflecting the old adage, "Sell on the news." But then it took off, breaking through resistance at about $35 and finishing the year at $40, near its all-time high.

Even after this runup, I felt Mobil was still an attractive bargain, and I remain optimistic today. Most of the bad news has been wrung out of the stock and management is in a strong position to pursue further restructuring steps that can help realize the company's present value of equity—$63 a share without any real improvement in oil and gas prices. Here are some of the streamlining efforts you should look for as an investor:

1. *The sale of Montgomery Ward or a spinoff to shareholders, especially now that it has become profitable after years of draining off billions in cash flow.* Management has vowed to do this by the end of 1988. This ultimate disposition has been anticipated for so long, and Montgomery Ward is such a small piece of Mobil, that the actual news will likely have more of a psychological value than any meaningful near-term impact on the stock price. But by removing this strategic weakness at Mobil—and the very symbol of poor diversification—management will be able to focus nearly all its enormous resources on the oil and gas business . . . especially if it were to take Step 2.

2. *Spin off the chemicals company to shareholders, or sell it, as USX did successfully with Aristech in 1986.* Chemicals has become a profitable business for Mobil, but it represents such a tiny segment of Mobil (about 5 percent of the $40 billion property

value) that investors aren't paying for that good performance in Mobil stock by bidding it higher.

3. *Separate refining and marketing from exploration and production.* Fortified by a famous trade name and well-regarded management, Mobil's downstream operations would be worth much more to current Mobil stockholders as a separate entity in the stock market.

4. *If management is unwilling to part with refining and marketing operations, it should at least create an independent company with a geographical segment of Mobil's oil and gas production business.* For example, Mobil is the second largest producer in the Kansas Hugoton (behind Amoco) and could easily create a pure play entity to hold all of its reserves there. This would appeal to institutional investors looking for a high-capitalization company focused on the Hugoton.

Even without major restructuring, Mobil still offers tremendous untapped value in its oil and gas resources. If you can buy the stock when it has a McDep of about .75 at the going rate ($8/$1.10), this means you're buying these underlying reserves for about 75% of their market value. That's the kind of long-term bet I like to make.

PHILLIPS PETROLEUM

Stock price, 10/19/87: $11.8
McDep ratio: .79
Yield: 5.1 percent

If you're reasonably optimistic about oil and gas prices, Phillips could offer a rewarding low-priced, low-McDep

106

opportunity, but with more implied risk than my other recommended integrated companies.

This risk/reward situation for investors stems from late 1984, when Phillips took on a staggering debt load to survive takeover attempts by T. Boone Pickens and Carl Icahn. Even after slashing operating costs and selling over $2 billion worth of assets to help pay off that debt, the company still had a debt-to-property ratio of .58 in mid-1987, highest of all the integrated companies. Debt ratios over .50 are worrisome when oil prices are declining; debt service costs can be significant and there is threatened loss of control to tenders. Yet when energy prices head upward, a high amount of debt gives a company like Phillips disproportionate financial leverage to the upside.

In fact, even after doubling from its mid-1986 lows near $8 a share, Phillips stock has as much long-term price appreciation potential as any oil stock, based on my McDep tables. If we look ahead several years to when I project the value of oil and gas in the ground at $12/bbl and $1.50/mcf, Phillips (based on an $18 stock price) projects to a .60 McDep ratio. It looks more compelling when we compare the ratios of current stock price to present value of equity (again, based on my future property value estimates). This is the technique I emphasized before creating McDep and it gives an advantage to high-debt companies in a bullish energy market. On this basis, Phillips has the most appreciation potential of any integrated company at 280%, followed by Unocal at 250%. (See table 5-A.)

Still concerned about a possible sustained downturn in oil prices, Phillips management seems to want to pay down debt even further and reduce the company's exposure to any industry downturn. But Phillips's debt-to-property ratio will certainly remain high enough through 1988 and

1989 to offer financial leverage. Moreover, in my view, dedicating a great proportion of cash flow to paying down that debt is not all bad; it lessens the chances of poor investment decisions in the area of exploration and production by forcing management to invest in areas that are most likely to pay off, while forgoing the kind of prolific spending that caused the industry so many woes in the late 1970s and early 1980s.

One important reason I'm willing to risk a long-term investment in Phillips (assuming a relatively low McDep ratio under current conditions) is the company's sensitivity to natural gas prices. When we compare Phillips's market cap to proven U.S. natural gas reserves, the resulting low ratio (second only to Unocal among the small integrated companies) means that it should respond well to changes in natural gas prices—and I'm bullish about that price trend.

However, I don't want to overplay the significance of natural gas to Phillips because of its heavy investment in the gas refining business. It happens to be the country's leading producer and processor of natural gas liquids (e.g., propane, butane, ethane), a barely profitable business with unexciting prospects under most oil and gas pricing scenarios.

Forced by the 1984 takeover attempts to scale back as a far-flung, diversified energy concern, Phillips has been concentrating on its basic business—oil and gas—while shifting production emphasis to the domestic side. Existing properties have average reserve-life indexes of eight years for oil and eleven years for gas. Management has given analysts a fairly optimistic impression that the company has hidden potential to book new reserves and that other reserves are understated or won't take much effort or expense to develop, but I don't have enough confidence in those projections to give them much emphasis in any "buy" recommendation.

In the end, within the McDep framework, you would buy Phillips as a reasonably sound, undervalued company that has strong cash flow and extra financial leverage provided by its high debt load. If the going rate of oil and gas in the ground can approach historic highs, then Phillips—at a McDep of 1.0—could be selling for $45 a share several years down the road. Few other oil and gas stocks have that kind of percentage appreciation potential.

TEXACO

Stock price, 10/19/87: $33
McDep ratio: .66
Dividend yield: Nil

If the bitter and historic Texaco-Pennzoil litigation remains unresolved by the time you read this book, Texaco stock should represent a compelling buy. In fact, even if you have to wait a while for the underlying payoff, here's a chance to invest in a major oil company at about 66 percent of its actual property value (based on its October 19, 1987, McDep ratio of .66). Texaco ought to be a $63 stock today and a $93 stock in 1990 if its McDep ratio were to be 1.0, if 1990 oil and gas values were to reach their former peak, and if the Pennzoil suit costs $1 billion. Each additional billion dollars would reduce Texaco's breakup value by $4 a share.

Texaco's nightmare, and today's investment opportunity, began in December 1985, when a Houston jury said the company should pay Pennzoil $12 billion because of

Texaco's "interference" in Pennzoil's aborted transaction to acquire Getty. Although the magnitude of the award defied common sense, it forced Texaco to opt for bankruptcy protection four months later, not because of faltering finances but to forestall Pennzoil's claims for those damages. Texaco's stock plunged as low as $27 (helped along by elimination of its healthy $3 annual dividend), rallied as high as $49 in mid-1987, and then declined once again in the absence of any out-of-court settlement.

Predicting the eventual outcome of legal issues sometimes requires an act of faith, but I'm willing to bet that patient Texaco investors will eventually be well rewarded when the Pennzoil judgment is resolved and no longer overhangs the stock. With Texaco's $34 billion in property values helping to protect your downside, the major risk is that your investment could lie relatively dormant for many months—perhaps even a year or two—if the two companies fail to reach a settlement and Texaco must then exhaust all of its appeals. Should the litigation run its full course over several years, I think that Texaco will be vindicated ultimately and that the amount of damages due to Pennzoil will be slight.

If you're going to build a position in Texaco, I'd encourage you to start soon and not try to outguess ongoing developments, for this is a situation where the old Wall Street adage could hold true: "Better to be six months too early than one day too late." A sudden out-of-court settlement or an unexpected takeover attempt could quickly send Texaco stock soaring beyond a price you're willing to pay.

Even after a Pennzoil settlement, though, I wouldn't necessarily rush to sell all my Texaco shares. Ever since the jury verdict was announced, I've regarded the case as a dramatic catalyst for the eventual restructuring of Texaco—either by existing management or a new owner from the outside. Texaco management has performed so poorly since 1971 (with the lowest total return of any large integrated company) that it will face intense pressure to undertake structural changes that are long overdue and would enable the stock to reflect more fully the value of properties. By failing to take any creative actions, management could risk a takeover attempt by large independent shareholders or a rival company such as Royal Dutch, Exxon, Atlantic Richfield, or Amoco (if it fails to acquire Dome Petroleum).

My own published reform program for Texaco would be to divide the company into eight or ten manageable pieces and let each piece run itself as a separate entity in the stock market. Management talent would surface in each piece and investors would tend to value each piece at close to a 1.0 McDep ratio. The cumulative value would far exceed the value of the original whole, especially as the oil and gas business continues to strengthen.

In a sense, we could do an AT&T on Texaco. Start by separating refining/marketing from exploration and production, and then create smaller entities in each of those functional areas. Even if as many as ten companies were created, the average size would still exceed $2 billion. Existing top management could run one of the newly created refining/marketing companies, preserving the company name.

We've seen how the eight regional Bell operating companies are all up more than 100 percent in stock market value since the AT&T divestiture in 1984. The same appreciation potential could be realized in the pieces of Texaco.

UNOCAL

Stock price, 10/19/87: $29
McDep ratio: .74
Yield: 3.5 percent

There are four basic reasons I favor an investment in Unocal, a company with tremendous untapped financial value.

1. *The company has a low McDep ratio, especially when we project toward 1990 and a return to historic oil and gas prices.* At $29, Unocal stock has a McDep of .56 under those conditions—higher only than Texaco and Amoco than five other integrated companies.

2. *Unocal's relatively high debt load gives the stock extra leverage as energy prices move higher.* The company's debt-to-property ratio (.49) is the second highest among major integrated companies (trailing only Phillips), suggesting the greatest potential percentage increase in stock value of any of these companies if oil and gas in the ground are valued at $12/bbl and $1.50/mcf. That debt created some discomfort when oil was going down in 1986, but now it can work in the stock's favor on the way back up. If our timing is good, buying Unocal stock today will be like buying a house with a low down payment and a big mortgage in a rising real estate market. Debt remains fixed in dollar terms, but the value of oil and gas reserves will be going up, meaning that Unocal's present value of equity will rise disproportionately—from $58 at today's values in the ground to $102 at my projected values.

Of course, this leverage factor will diminish in

the next several years as management continues to pay down debt and protect itself against unexpected downside reversals in oil and gas prices. Although debt repayment has siphoned off great hunks of Unocal's cash flow since the company fought off Mesa's takeover attempt in 1985, this has not necessarily been bad in the eyes of many investors. These constraints on capital spending have provided an effective discipline for management, forcing them to invest cash flow more efficiently than in the past and—logically, at least—to pursue only the best projects.

3. *Natural gas reserves are Unocal's most important source of future stock-price appreciation potential.* With 30 percent of its property value represented by U.S. natural gas reserves—the highest concentration of any major integrated company—Unocal is a standout in terms of sensitivity to natural gas prices. And I'm bullish on that pricing outlook. Another virtue here is that Unocal has long-life gas reserves (a fifteen-year reserve-life index), which give me greater confidence about holding on for a long-term payoff in the stock.

Nor is there anything mythical about the value of Unocal's gas properties, for they are highlighted separately in Union Exploration Partners, the limited partnership that holds all of Unocal's natural gas properties in the Gulf of Mexico. This pure play partnership had a premium McDep ratio of 1.28 in mid-August 1987, reflecting the potential value of all of Unocal's oil and gas reserves if they were held in a partnership or corporation form, independent of Unocal's overly diversified integrated structure.

4. *Management has the ability, if not the inclination, to do some creative restructuring that would boost Unocal stock much closer to its present value of equity at a faster rate.* I've long argued that Unocal is unnecessarily diversified at the expense of current shareholders, burying billions of dollars in assets that are underappreciated by stock market investors. In fact, in 1986 I even submitted a shareholder proposal at the annual meeting, suggesting that Unocal should be split into ten pieces to bring out the company's underlying value. I doubt there will be any major restructuring changes as long as Fred Hartley is chairman; he has built his empire over several decades and seems loath to part with any of the pieces. He even gambled the company's survival in 1986, refusing to sell off any properties to reduce a dangerous debt-to-property ratio as oil prices tumbled. Fortunately the oil market bottomed and turned upward just in time, from which point Unocal stock virtually tripled over the next year (from about $15 to about $45).

Nevertheless, while Unocal remains a solid, attractive buying opportunity without any restructuring, I'm not shy about suggesting ways that management could bring out submerged values without necessarily weakening the company. For example:

- Spin off Molycorp as an independent minerals company, as Amoco did with Cyprus Minerals and Pennzoil did with Battle Mountain Gold.
- Create an independent chemicals company.
- Spin off a geothermal company to highlight one of Unocal's gems. Unocal leads the industry in geothermal

energy production, which is quite profitable, but at present these operations are lost within Unocal's integrated structure. They have an estimated property value of $1.5 billion but contribute only about 10 percent of Unocal's total earnings.

■ Get a bit more adventurous by creating a West Coast exploration and production company that would own valuable reserves of enhanced recovery oil in California, similar to Chevron's extensive holdings.

■ European and Far East exploration and production operations could also be independent.

Successful implementation of restructuring steps like these would enable patient investors to reap healthy gains out of Unocal stock, while leaving existing management still in charge of a major energy company.

CHAPTER 5

THE COMING PAYOFF IN NATURAL GAS STOCKS

As an investment analyst, I spend a lot of time on the phone with institutional clients and various sources in the oil and gas business. I also log many hours every week reading about the industry, writing research reports, and updating my statistical data via my two computers. Yet the ongoing success of all this work depends to an important degree on my ability to sense a developing trend and then find the companies that are best positioned to take advantage of this trend.

I can get a good idea about trends just working in my basement office at home, but I've also found that it's crucial to travel periodically and meet the people who manage the companies I'm interested in and who produce the statistics that are so important to my evaluative work. What I find particularly useful about meeting these people face-to-face is that I can draw some conclusions about how convincing they seem to be and whether or not I trust them. I try to sense, "Can I rely on this person's insights? Can I trust his or her judgments?"

I gained that feeling of confidence through a chance meeting with oilman Al Wiederkehr out in Arizona in 1973, and it sparked my interest in a company that would eventually lead to several of the recommended stocks featured later in this chapter.

I was still a relative rookie in the business when I attended the 1973 Interstate Natural Gas Association convention in Scottsdale, shortly before the Arab oil boycott in October, but I knew in advance that I wanted to learn more about Aztec, a producer in the San Juan Basin of New Mexico. I had been following the company and I was intent on meeting the president, Quilly Davis, to see what he was like. So when I spotted him during a coffee break between sessions, I went up and introduced myself. He in turn introduced me to his friend, Al Wiederkehr, who was chairman of Supron (then known as Southern Union Production), another small but promising producer with long-lived natural gas reserves in the San Juan Basin. The three of us talked a bit and I liked them both. I was also intrigued by what Wiederkehr had to say about his company's prospects, and when I returned to New York I added it to the stocks I was following.

I continued to stay abreast of Aztec and Supron, but not until May 1975 was I ready to make them official "buy" recommendations. They were good ideas in late 1973, but also inappropriate risks in the investment environment at that time. As I learned early from my colleagues and my own experience, one of the challenges in being a successful stock analyst is having the necessary patience to sit on a good idea until the timing is opportune and resist the temptation to rush into print too soon with a "buy" recommendation.

One reason I delayed taking action with Aztec and Supron was that gas stocks had already fared well in 1973. And as we moved into 1974, the oil embargo was sending the economy into a sharp recession and causing the stock market to slump toward a bear-market low in September. In an environment like that, I tended to emphasize the larger integrated oil companies (Phillips and Marathon were two successful picks) while avoiding the smaller, more vulnerable exploration companies and producers. By the spring of 1975, however, I was far more optimistic about the prospects for natural gas, and in May I published a "buy" recommendation on all nine of the independent natural gas exploration companies, including Aztec and Supron. I clearly had a feeling these stocks were ready to take off, based on the industry's improving political and economic outlook.

Supron was selling for $20 at the time—though actually only $2 when adjusted for subsequent stock splits. I liked it for three main reasons: (1) a deserved reputation for management skill, (2) impressive long-life gas reserves in the San Juan Basin, and (3) its built-in potential to produce much more gas at much higher prices. I noted that most of Supron's gas was regulated at below-market prices, meaning the company was receiving an extremely low average wellhead price for the gas it produced. I was willing to bet that eventually the price of this gas would be worth considerably more through infill drilling in the San Juan Basin. Under Federal regulations, producers were allowed to charge a much higher price for gas produced by the drilling of new wells. Infill drilling would also allow Supron to increase reserves in existing properties without having to invest in heavy exploration expenses.

Eventually this all came about and rewarded patient investors in spectacular fashion. New Mexico regulators allowed infill drilling, Supron raised the wellhead price it received for its gas, and its reserves were continually raised over time—while the market price for gas rose to record levels.

My continuing friendly relationship with Supron's CEO, Al Wiederkehr, was an important factor in my long-term success with the stock. He was always enthusiastic about his company and helpful about keeping me up-to-date, which helped fortify my confidence in Supron. For example, the crucial infill-drilling idea in the San Juan Basin had to be approved by New Mexico officials, and Al was particularly good at keeping me informed about ongoing political developments. This was important input, for if I could be confident that New Mexico would eventually approve infill drilling (which it did starting in 1979), then I could aggressively recommend the stock to patient though hesitant investors.

In 1976, for instance, I noted that Supron was a relatively tiny company in the oil and gas universe (like the Dorchester Hugoton of today, as we'll see), but that "shareholders have a valuable asset that should become better recognized." My confidence in Supron's future payoff potential was given a boost that year when one of my early "ideas," Aztec, was acquired by Southland Royalty for a surprisingly high price.

Given the fact that regulatory developments turned out to be amazingly positive, coupled with skyrocketing oil and gas prices, it shouldn't be surprising that Supron would eventually perform in spectacular fashion. The party ended on a high note when Supron was acquired by Allied Corporation and Continental Group for $35 a share in May 1982, completing a seventeenfold appreciation in the seven years since my recommendation. A combination of under-valued properties that provided continuing volume growth, natural gas increases, and excellent management contributed to this success as investors focused on periodically higher asset values. Supron had high-quality natural gas properties, but management resisted the temptation to squander this tremendous asset base on acquisitions of unrelated businesses. Instead, it actually shrunk the size of the company by buying back stock and shedding its former parent, Southern Union Production. This created a purer natural gas company that would tend to sell closer to asset value, as we've seen with McDep. Management was also oriented to the shareholders. Acknowledging that there was a price at which it was in the best interest of shareholders to sell, management recommended acceptance of the $35 cash offer—when gas prices were virtually at their peak.

KN ENERGY: A WORTHY SUCCESSOR TO SUPRON

The Supron acquisition was actually announced in October 1981, and shortly after that I was again attending the INGA convention in Arizona. My wife, Louise, delayed appearing at the closing cocktail party, but I decided to attend early, not knowing who I might meet or what I might learn. When Louise arrived I told her, "I've got another Supron."

The company that caught my fancy was Kansas-Nebraska Natural Gas (known today as KN Energy). This pipeline company had significant gas reserves in the Hugoton field of Kansas and some of the same characteristics of Supron many years earlier: that is, production with an extremely low average wellhead price and the potential for infill drilling. Investors had started thinking about infill drilling in the Hugoton late in 1979 when Mesa Petroleum formed Mesa Royalty Trust, whose gas reserves were in the Hugoton field and San Juan Basin. Infill drilling was already benefiting San Juan producers, but the country's largest gas field, the Hugoton, remained underdeveloped.

By the time of the INGA convention in 1981, Mesa's Boone Pickens had been actively trying to make investors aware of the potential for infill drilling in Kansas. At that final cocktail party, I found myself talking with Elmer Jackson, chief counsel of KN Energy, and Jack Byrd, a lawyer for Mesa in Kansas. I mentioned that the campaign for infill drilling in the Hugoton seemed to be gathering steam, though it still faced considerable opposition by the Kansas Corporation Commission, the determining body. What struck me at that point was Elmer Jackson's reaction as Jack Byrd elaborated a bit about infill politics. Elmer is a cagey guy, but he seemed surprised that the issue had become active in Kansas and was genuinely unenthusiastic about infill drilling's eventual impact on Kansas-Nebraska's pipeline operation. After all, the company would be forced to pay much higher prices for this "new" gas from other Hugoton producers, as opposed to "old" gas from fields in production before 1977—a price difference of about 8-to-1 at the time.

My instinct, however, was to realize how much infill drilling would benefit the producing segments of KN Energy, far more than it would hurt pipeline profits. Knowing how infill drilling had been a boon for Supron in the San Juan Basin, I was convinced that similar drilling would have an equally positive impact on Hugoton producers—by allowing them to greatly increase their production at considerably higher prices, while strengthening their reserves.

When I returned to New York, I added Kansas-Nebraska to my research coverage and I began placing a higher probability on the potential for natural gas decontrol and the growing likelihood that producers in the Kansas Hugoton would eventually realize far more value from their production there. Eventually, in March 1982, I formally recommended Kansas-Nebraska at $22 a share. I cited the company's sizable reserves in the Hugoton field, the prospect for infill drilling "within a few years," and the promise of price decontrols on natural gas. I felt that the Hugoton would eventually be a carbon copy of developments in the San Juan Basin and that Kansas-Nebraska, with the lowest average wellhead price, had the most to gain. I had screened sixty oil and gas companies and KN was "the most promising bargain." Although none of the mechanisms for substantially increasing the pricing of KN's valuable gas reserves were entirely assured, "the prospects for relief appear bright," I wrote. "In view of our experience with Supron, where there was no greater assurance seven years ago, the investment attractiveness of Kansas-Nebraska appears to rate very high." I also speculated at the time that KN management might find it desirable to separate much of its production operations from utility operations, following the lead of several other companies.

Indeed, that's exactly what transpired at KN Energy. First, as a defensive measure to discourage a threatened takeover, the company spun off Midlands Energy to stockholders in September 1983. Midlands opened at $19 a share and within a year was acquired by Freeport McMoRan for $26. (Midlands held nearly all of KN's oil and gas reserves outside the Hugoton field.) Two years later, in September 1985, KN Energy created another independent entity in Plains Petroleum, which held the company's prime Hugoton reserves. Spun off on a 1-to-1 share basis to shareholders, Plains had an opening-day price of $20—higher than its parent, which closed at $17.

This successful restructuring by KN Energy management helps bolster my argument on behalf of deintegration at the major oil companies. Here we had a management that adroitly created two original pieces that could be appreciated in the stock market and could bring out previously unrealized value for shareholders. Meanwhile, a management skilled in running a regulated business—a pipeline company—still controlled the business it knew best.

Ultimately, the investor who bought Kansas-Nebraska stock at the time of my original recommendation in 1982 (at $22)—and held on—would have realized $26 through the Midlands Energy spinoff and subsequent acquisition; $17 in KN Energy at the time of the Plains spinoff (I recommended that clients sell their KN shares and shift into Plains as a pure play on Hugoton gas production); and $24 in Plains at year-end 1986. The total resulting value of these three pieces: $67 plus a good dividend at KN Energy, or a threefold gain. Ironically, this payoff never fully reflected the long-anticipated benefits of infill drilling in the Hugoton field of Kansas. Not until 1986 did the Kansas Corporation Commission give its approval for additional drilling, but one of the immediate beneficiaries was Plains Petroleum—a piece of the original whole. I'll provide a closer look at this company later in the chapter.

WHY NATURAL GAS STOCKS BELONG IN YOUR PORTFOLIO

Watching—patiently—as the natural gas industry recovers from many years of declining fortunes, I'm confident that gas capacity (supply) and current consumption (demand) will inevitably come in balance again, perhaps as early as 1988. Unlike oil, natural gas production in this country is below capacity, reflecting lagging demand, and that capacity is declining every day because we're not replacing reserves. This means that capacity will inevitably drop to the current demand level and eliminate the notorious gas "bubble," thus bringing about sharply higher prices and escalating property values for the best-positioned natural gas producers.

Before I highlight my favorite companies, let's analyze why your McDep Energy Fund should contain at least one natural gas producer with long-life reserves and one integrated company with significant gas properties. Now's the time to start building a position in this crucial area of the U.S. energy business so that you can fully participate in the gas industry's recovery and subsequent boom period.

1. *Natural gas represents a "safer," more stable investment than oil.* My reasoning here is that the market price for gas is not as volatile as the oil price—and volatility is a measure of risk. While the average oil price plunged 50 percent in 1986, from $26 to $13 a barrel, the average wellhead price for gas dropped by only 25 percent, from $2.60 to $2 per mcf.

Oil also carries a higher political risk than gas,

since the price can be held hostage by world developments and government actions. Moreover, while the United States will grow increasingly dependent on OPEC oil, we can continue to meet nearly all our gas production needs many years into the future. Even though natural gas represents about a third of our total energy needs, we can control the production, distribution, and access right here. Again, that implies less risk and more predictability.

Yet at the same time, natural gas will gain additional appreciation potential through its strategic value as an alternative to imported oil—particularly if oil imports are interrupted or curtailed for any length of time.

2. *Natural gas has a more predictable future than oil.* From an industry growth standpoint, for example, there are far more opportunities to develop future gas reserves than oil reserves within the United States. Very clearly, undiscovered gas reserves greatly exceed those for oil, meaning greater production potential and more assured earnings growth.

United States companies produce all the oil they can find today, and they won't be finding much new oil inside U.S. borders in the near future. But we know we're going to find all the natural gas we will need, especially by increasing production in major gas properties where the gas is ''shut in'' or deliberately underproduced and by going into existing fields such as the Hugoton and the San Juan Basin to implement infill drilling. There are far fewer such prospects for drilling the oil wells needed to replace current oil production. Nor are we yet dependent on finding major new gas fields, as there are many potential areas we already know about, plus the possibilities of more discoveries. Vast areas considered gas prone still remain unexplored, while some huge (though presently uneconomical) discoveries have already been made in the Overthrust Belt of Colorado and Wyoming.

3. *Natural gas responds well to higher oil prices, but is not entirely dependent on these prices for industry success.* For example, as oil becomes more expensive and harder to find, oil demand will go down in response to pricing competition (e.g., with natural gas and coal) and conservation measures. Yet these higher oil prices help make natural gas a more desirable commodity for use by industrial outfits such as electrical power plants. And when the price of oil can remain above $20 a barrel, residual fuel oil becomes less competitive with gas, which helps gas demand expand—and thus its pricing outlook.

4. *The reserve-life index of gas is much longer than for oil, offering investors greater long-term security.* We measure oil and gas reserves by a ratio of proven reserves to annual production: for example, barrels of reserves divided by barrels of production each year. This yields a reserve-life index. A fourteen-year reserve-life index means that existing reserves will actually last about twenty-eight years, produced at a declining yearly rate. Obviously a long reserve-life index is desirable, signaling to investors that a company has already found sufficient reserves for production over the near term but will still have plenty of reserves remaining well into the future, when gas should be priced much higher. By buying long-life U.S. reserves today, you can rest comfortably with a long-term perspective.

The search for long-life reserves leads inevitably to natural gas because there are few existing oil properties in the United States that are not already in advanced stages of depletion. Few companies offer long-life oil reserves, since oil is produced to capacity in this country and we're not finding significant amounts of new oil to improve a bleak reserve situation. The only oil in place that appears to have a notably long reserve life is the famous Yates field in Texas, one of the jewels held by USX (through Marathon). The field is producing at about a twenty-year reserve-life index versus an oil industry average of about eight or nine years.

These realities in the oil business automatically highlight long-life natural gas properties. My favorite gas stocks, in fact, have a reserve-life index of fourteen to twenty-six years. They include Plains (twenty-two years), Dorchester (twenty-one), Consolidated Oil and Gas (twenty-one), Anadarko (twenty-two), Wiser (fourteen), Southwestern Energy (twenty), San Juan Basin Royalty Trust (twenty-six), Mesa Limited Partnership (eighteen), and Burlington Northern (seventeen) as a diversified railroad/energy play.

You may be thinking, "Why do I need to worry about reserves so far down the road? Can't I make good money over the next year or two with companies that have only short-lived oil and gas reserves?"

Well, it's true that a company's reserve-life index may not prove crucial to the shorter-term investor, but you limit your potential gain while injecting greater downside risk when you buy companies with poor-quality reserves (meaning those lower than the industry average). These figures are supplied in the Appendix on page 195.)

When the oil and gas outlook is improving, and especially if there's a strong upside move, the short-life companies can do well—but the long-life companies will do even better. Investors perceive the long-life companies as stronger, better-positioned entities with greater stock appreciation potential as wellhead prices rise. People buying these companies are acquiring reserves they feel confident will be worth considerably more when they are produced in the future.

Also beware of the reverse situation that can prevail if energy prices trend downward. Investors are understandably fearful of a company with just a five-year reserve life in oil, since about half of its reserves might be produced within two or three years. The challenge to replace these reserves is also greater for the short-life company. If oil prices are declining, not only does this diminish the amount of cash flow available for exploration and production, but a company producing 20 percent of its reserves in a year must replace 20 percent, as compared to a company that is producing just 5 percent of its reserves. On balance, it is easier to replace a smaller percentage of reserves than a larger percentage.

5. *Even if you never buy an independent natural gas producer or a trust or partnership with significant gas reserves,* you should stay abreast of developments in the industry and appreciate the values that exist, for natural gas represents an important position at integrated companies such as Amoco, Texaco, Mobil, Unocal, and Phillips.

A BULLISH PRICE TREND FOR NATURAL GAS

Coming into 1987, I felt that natural gas had uncertain near-term prospects as the industry recovered from a cyclical bottom. But I was quite confident about prospects for the gas business in 1988 and beyond, sensing that we were heading for a shortage that could prove to be quite severe. I still feel that way, convinced that sometime over the next year or two, gas prices are going to move sharply higher, taking gas-oriented stocks with them.

One reason I can build an aggressive long-term case for natural gas is the fact that the industry was steadily undermined from 1981 through 1986 by a surplus of supply (the infamous gas "bubble"), weak consumption, and declining prices. As a result, there is still excess daily capacity in the U.S. gas system, meaning there's more gas available for production and delivery than there is demand. This in turn has kept prices restrained, helped along by the slump in oil prices in 1986. These forces, however, are now helping to close the gap—somewhat inexorably—between capacity and demand. Although demand may remain roughly flat in 1987, as compared to 1986, overall capacity is declining daily because we're not replacing our natural gas reserves. The resources are there, but economic factors keep them from being produced, thus hastening eventual shortages.

Since a gas surplus has plagued the industry since 1981, drilling has declined sharply, hitting record low levels in June 1986. As a result, producers replaced only an estimated 74 percent of 1985 production and also fell short in 1986. This percentage could drop even lower in 1987. With little new production coming on stream, our surplus gas capacity is steadily declining as we basically live off our existing reserves. We still have plenty of capacity to meet immediate demand—just "pull down" the wells a little harder and produce at a faster rate—but eventually capacity and demand will come together and cause gas prices to move higher. Even before that gap actually closes, prices will begin firming as buyers and sellers perceive a tight market looming.

Another factor that has been restraining natural gas prices and helping to postpone a gas shortage in the United States has been the increased availability of gas from Canada in recent years. There's sufficient pipeline capacity to bring in about 8 percent of our total annual consumption from Canada. We've only been importing about 4 percent a year, leaving a potential supply in Canada, but once we reach that 8 percent level, more pipelines will have to be built—at considerable cost—to bring in more gas. In addition, remember that the Canadian gas business is also emerging from a depressed era that has severely curtailed drilling, and these producers are not prepared to flood the U.S. market and keep gas prices at a continual low level.

We tend to view Canada as a gas competitor, which it is to an extent, but ultimately we need a portion of its gas and the assurance of its future reserves (which represent about half the U.S. reserves) in order to have a healthy, stable industry.

Why is this so? Well, U.S. gas producers must increase demand by opening up new markets for gas so that they can drain off today's excess producing capacity. We're certainly not taking advantage of all the opportunities to use more natural gas in the country, but before major new users (e.g., electric utility plants) will commit to conversion from other fuel sources, management needs the assurance of a consistent gas supply many years into the future at a reasonable price. Some of these potential buyers are skeptical that current depressed prices will last very long and they fear an eventual price squeeze in the U.S. market. So my feeling is that U.S. producers, in cooperation with Canadian producers, can work out appropriate agreements to meet these supply and pricing requirements and thus remove potential barriers to expanded demand for natural gas.

Another reason I'm projecting a positive price trend for natural gas is the improving outlook for oil prices. No one factor determines the course of gas pricing, but oil is certainly the most important influence.

For example, when oil prices drop significantly, as they did in 1986, residual fuel oil—the dregs of the barrel—becomes more appealing to large-scale, low-quality applications such as power plants. At this level, natural gas must compete exclusively on a heating basis with residual fuel oil and it gets no premium in price for its convenience or cleanliness. The popularity of residual fuel oil thus limits large-scale demand for gas and thus helps depress its price.

However, as the price of oil moves higher (especially above $15), residual fuel oil becomes more expensive and less competitive with gas, even without a change in the gas price. Home heating oil also becomes less competitive. This helps expand gas demand and prompts conversions from oil back to natural gas. We're seeing this now as industrial users who switched to burning oil in their plants in 1986 are moving back to gas. In fact, a sizable chunk of the industrial market—25 percent or so—can switch between oil and gas, depending on the price trend.

Improved economic activity and a pickup in industrial production will also boost demand for natural gas and help shrink the surplus of production capacity. Meanwhile, the wellhead price for gas will move up to restore a normal degree of interfuel competition—but at higher overall price levels.

My optimism for natural gas prospects is bolstered by the fact that several of my rival analysts are rather unexcited about industry fundamentals through 1990. They forecast a continued era of sluggish demand, ample supplies, and only slightly improved prices. I think this is a complacent view, downplaying the fact that economic trends involving commodities rarely proceed that smoothly; we either go to one extreme or the other. Now that we're finally coming off a long extreme on the downside, I'm convinced we're headed for an extreme on the upside as we work through 1988 and 1989. In fact, any sharp upward turn in natural gas prices will catch a lot of buyers off guard, adding even greater momentum to those prices as buyers scramble to work out long-term contracts with producers and lessen their current dependence on the spot market.

So before other investors go on a buying spree for natural gas stocks, stake a position in several of the stocks that I'll now be highlighting—and then sit tight. Some of these companies may appear quite small, especially if you're accustomed to investing in large capitalization stocks, and may seem too obscure if you like to read something about your stocks in the newspapers and magazines every so often. But with natural gas prices finally on the rebound, it makes sense to buy the companies with the purest representation in natural gas production and long-life reserves—whatever the company's size or public recognition—so that you can participate in the growing value of those reserves. McDep will help you identify the best investments.

PLAINS PETROLEUM

Stock price, 10/29/87: $22
McDep ratio: .64
Yield: .2 percent

I've been recommending Plains Petroleum since its spinoff from KN Energy as an independent production company in September 1985. Starting at $19 a share, Plains stock topped $33 early in 1987 before settling around $30. I'm confident there's sizable appreciation potential ahead as various factors coalesce.

The most important, unwavering factor in Plains's future is the fact that it represents the purest possible investment in the vast Hugoton gas field of southwest Kansas. The Hugoton, which also stretches across parts of Texas and Oklahoma, is the largest gas field in the contiguous United States, rivaled only by the Prudhoe Bay field in Alaska. (Prudhoe has more natural gas in one place, but its potential value is negated by the high cost of transportation.)

Reserves in the Hugoton are not only long-life and easily accessible, but are being produced at far less than capacity. Coupled with rising gas prices, Plains thus offers a powerful combination of forces, allowing you to participate in the value of these natural gas resources decades into the future, building from today's relatively low prices. Here are other important points to keep in mind:

1. *Infill drilling will allow Plains to continue expanding its low-cost reserves at increasingly higher prices.* Until 1987, the Hugoton was only partially developed at one well per square mile; Kansas regulations will now allow producers eventually to drill four wells per square mile. At Plains, if we assume that

133

reserve estimates will prove to be greater than anticipated, and assuming that the price of gas can return to its 1981 peak, then we're looking at impressive potential in Plains stock.

2. *Cash flow will increase rapidly throughout 1987 and 1988 as Plains's wellhead price for natural gas approaches the industry average.* A key breakthrough came in 1986 when Plains reached a new contract agreement with its purchaser, KN Energy, agreeing to a wellhead price of about $1.60/mcf for its 1987 production—more than double its previous level of $.70 (a price that had been held far below the industry average by price controls). Equally important, the renegotiated contract has an annual "reopener" clause, providing a new year-ahead price based on the industry's average spot price. This negotiated price has already been set at $1.60/mcf for 1988, but should certainly move up steadily in subsequent years.

3. *Plains started paying a small dividend in 1987, but I expect that they will continue to reinvest cash flow mostly in oil and gas reserves.* Eventually there could be a large dividend payout as infill drilling phases out in the early 1990s.

4. *Plains represents an attractive acquisition candidate.* It's a simple, easily digested company in that all it does is produce natural gas. Thus, a natural acquirer would be a company that wants to shore up its natural gas business.

5. *Although a lot of good near-term news came out on Plains in 1986 and 1987, the stock still remains undervalued and doesn't fully reflect the potential of its Hugoton reserves coupled with stronger gas prices.* Early in 1987, when I raised my estimates of gas in

the ground from $.90 to $1.10/mcf, the present value of Plains equity went from $30 to $37, and I felt the stock had appreciation potential to $40 by late 1987. Looking further ahead, Plains should be compared to high-quality exploration companies or limited partnerships that trade on Wall Street at ten times cash flow. Since Plains's future cash flow might be $5 a share sometime in the future, the implication is a $52 stock price or better (based on my $12/$1.50 tables). McDep could add conviction here if Plains continues to remain at or near the bottom of the group of large U.S. oil and gas production companies.

Acknowledging that there is no perfect store of value, whether it is bank accounts or real estate, Plains Petroleum is an attractive possession to be held for a long time.

DORCHESTER HUGOTON

Stock price, 10/29/87: $14
McDep ratio: .86
Yield: 1.3 percent

I have been recommending this limited partnership since March 1983, when it was selling for $3 (adjusted for a 3-for-1 split in October, 1987). The stock rose to $5 by year-end 1985, reached $8 a year later as anticipated developments came to pass, and then doubled from there to $16. Even at that price level, Dorchester had a McDep ratio near the bottom of the trusts and partnerships group.

There's still considerable long-term potential left in

this little gem and I'm confident it will prove to be a great buy for the patient investor. The only real drawback is that we don't know *when* two favorable decisions—expected but not guaranteed—will occur and bring out much more of Dorchester's enormous potential. But my experience with Supron and KN Energy, where similar regulatory actions fell into place, makes a powerful case for Dorchester. Here are the key factors in that appreciation potential:

1. *Dorchester offers pure representation in high-quality Hugoton gas reserves that have a reserve-life index of twenty-one years*. There's plenty of secure value with gas reserves that can be produced so far into the future at potentially higher prices. In fact, Dorchester has more natural gas reserves relative to stock market value than any other financially strong oil and gas company.

2. *About 20 percent of Dorchester's reserves are in the Kansas Hugoton field, where it is now benefiting from infill drilling and price deregulation, the same as Plains*. Earnings or cash flow could double in 1987 as Dorchester renegotiates contracts and improves the wellhead price of its Kansas gas from about $.40/mcf to the industry average of about $1.70/mcf.

3. *The remaining 80 percent of Dorchester's properties are in the Oklahoma Hugoton, where it still receives abnormally low wellhead prices for its gas (less than $.70/mcf) and infill drilling is not yet allowed*. This combination restrains current production and earnings, but also represents the untapped, under-recognized future potential at Dorchester.

Potential infill drilling in Oklahoma represents about 40 percent of Dorchester's overall production capacity. The various Oklahoma producers (including Phillips and Mobil) are working to gain approval for this drilling, which would allow production to be priced close to the industry average. Regulatory proceedings grind slowly, as we learned in Kansas, but I expect the Oklahoma Corporation Commission to follow its neighbor's lead, as it has done in the past.

Dorchester must also renegotiate a fixed-price contract with Midcon, its pipeline distributor, so that it can receive a higher wellhead price in Oklahoma for the remaining 40 percent of its gas production. Midcon is owned by Occidental and the gas produced by Dorchester actually accounts for just a miniscule amount of Midcon's throughput.

4. *Dorchester may be able to double its potential reserves in the coming years through infill drilling in Oklahoma and a recovery technique called "fracturing."* This treatment involves pumping fluids underground at high pressure to break up the existing formations. Sometimes this technique simply causes the gas to flow out faster, but more often it begins to flow from new zones, enhancing the amount of potential reserves. Many wells in the Hugoton were drilled thirty or more years ago, but nothing has been done to them in the way of recovering "lost" or untapped reserves and thus increasing production capacity.

5. *Dorchester's dividend yield is tiny compared to other trusts and partnerships, but has been steadily improving and could eventually represent a sizable payout.* Many investors look to trusts and partnerships for their dividend yield as well as a play on oil and gas prospects and thus are unwilling to pay too

high a price for Dorchester stock. Most people simply don't understand its future potential well enough and will need to be convinced. Current cash flow is tiny, but not that relevant to what the potential will be as events in Oklahoma unfold. So one positive step in this regard will come when investors can anticipate a much higher dividend payout that reflects Dorchester's rapidly increasing cash flow. Limited partnerships normally pay out most of their cash flow to unit holders.

6. *Low-priced gas properties make Dorchester a prime takeover possibility.* Though long-term investors stand to reap greater profits through an independent Dorchester, the partnership would represent an outstanding investment for an operating company that has been having lackluster exploration results in natural gas and wants to spend money for reserves. Just a sliver of the capital budget for a modest-sized company could purchase all of Dorchester (which has an estimated property value of just $90 million) and would do wonders for its exploration effort. Ideally, Dorchester should be targeted by a major company that has other relationships with Midcon, thereby easing renegotiation of the Oklahoma pricing contract.

Ultimately, Dorchester Hugoton's stock has considerably more upside potential than Plains Petroleum, but greater uncertainty about how soon that potential can be realized. However, we've seen the progress with infill drilling in Kansas (representing about 20 percent of the partnership's production) and I'm confident that infill drilling will be allowed in Oklahoma and that the contract with Midcon ultimately will be renegotiated. The question is when these restraints will be lifted. If you find that Dorchester's latest stock price hasn't improved much over the price given here, that's a good indication that progress still lies ahead.

Here's one way to view Dorchester's potential. Right now it has natural gas reserves of about 26 mcf a share (a figure I obtain by dividing reserves by the number of units or shares outstanding). If we look down the road and assume that natural gas in the ground could be worth $1.50 again by 1990, as it was at the last peak in 1981, then 26 mcf times $1.50 would represent a stock worth about $39. That's powerful long-term potential for anybody's portfolio, but you must squirrel the stock away and wait for the ultimate payoff, which could be even higher than my projections. For example, if Dorchester can indeed increase present reserves by 50 percent through infill drilling and other developments, then it would eventually have 40 mcf per unit—or a stock worth $60 with a going rate for gas in the ground of $1.50 mcf.

While it's always hard visualizing a stock performing that well, just remember Supron's seventeenfold gain.

CONSOLIDATED OIL AND GAS

Stock price, 10/29/87: $1.75
McDep ratio: .74
Yield: Nil

This is my blue-plate special, a $3 stock that has more appreciation *potential* than any other of the one hundred companies covered by my McDep analysis. I've projected a fivefold gain (to $14 a share) if the stock achieves a McDep ratio of 1.0, based on my 1990 estimates of oil valued at $12 in the ground and natural gas at $1.50/mcf.

Consolidated Oil and Gas (not to be confused with the pipeline company, Consolidated Natural Gas) is a pure play in natural gas, with high-quality properties in the San Juan Basin (reserve-life index: twenty-one years) that offer volume growth as gas prices improve and demand rises. Moreover, a small amount of market cap ($31 million) controls a surprising amount of property value ($140 million) as compared to a company like Plains, which has $290 million market cap controlling $390 million of property value. I'll describe presently how this helps give Consolidated tremendous financial leverage as natural gas recovers.

The caveat here is that Consolidated has a dangerous but manageable debt-to-property ratio of .64. This high debt, coupled with declining gas prices, drove the stock to below $1 at the end of 1986 (down from $25). But by March, with oil prices clearly on the rebound, the company had managed to escape bankruptcy and I felt the stock (then about $1½) offered speculative appeal.

Consolidated's powerful appreciation potential goes beyond an improving natural gas environment, owing to a combination of financial and operational leverage. Briefly, here's how that leverage could work, comparing Consolidated and Plains and presuming that as gas prices rise, the percentage change in valuation will be the same for both companies.

At Plains, if property value goes up 50 percent (based on my 1990 estimates), $390 million would increase to $570 million, and that increment—$18 a share—would accrue to stockholders, because debt doesn't change in these calculations (and Plains has no debt). Bottom line, Plains stock would improve from $32 to $50.

Roughly the same thing occurs at Consolidated, except that with a 50 percent increase in property value ($140 million to $210 million) the increment increase of $7 would more than triple the value of the stock to $10.

The potential pitfall at Consolidated remains debt, and you should keep this risk in mind if you make a big commitment. But I think the risk/reward ratio is attractive. Also keep in mind that the company was contemplating a rights offering in late 1987, which would improve Consolidated's financial condition but lower my property estimates.

OTHER PROMISING NATURAL GAS PRODUCERS

As industry trends keep improving, I've been emphasizing other well-managed, well-positioned producers beyond Plains and Dorchester Hugoton that should benefit most from higher natural gas prices. There's Mesa Limited Partnership, of course, which will eventually profit from infill drilling and price deregulation in the Hugoton field of Kansas. (I'll cover Mesa, as well as two favorite royalty trusts, Permian Basin and San Juan Basin, in Chapter 6.) Other recommendations, keeping the McDep technique in mind, include:

ANADARKO PETROLEUM
Stock price, 10/29/87: $23
McDep ratio: .95
Yield: 1.3 percent

Spun off from Panhandle Eastern in 1986, Anadarko is a premier production company with 86 percent of its estimated property value in natural gas that has a superb reserve-life index of twenty-two years. Unless the stock price weakens, Anadarko represents a fully valued stock in terms of McDep but offers a strategic commitment to gas reserves that will still be ample when future prices are much higher than they are today. Half of these reserves are in the Kansas Hugoton, where the company will be benefiting from infill drilling and a deregulation of "old" (thus low-priced) natural gas prices. Regulatory changes will allow Anadarko's average price realization to rise toward the industry average. Another one-third of the company's gas reserves are represented by the Matagorda Island development offshore of Texas.

Many institutional investors are willing to pay a premium McDep for Anadarko because of its greater public recognition (as compared to Plains and Dorchester) and their confidence in management. In fact, among the pure plays in oil and gas production, Anadarko is the largest corporation concentrated on long-life natural gas.

As you research Anadarko, don't be misled by the company's low book value, since the Hugoton reserves are listed at a nominal number, far below their actual value, even at today's gas prices. Their book value of reserves is $1.2 billion as compared to my estimated present value of $1.8 billion.

WISER OIL

Stock price, 10/29/87: $15
McDep ratio: .61
Yield: 2.7 percent

You very likely have never heard of Wiser Oil, an independent production company headquartered in Sistersville, West Virginia. True, Wiser is just a peanut in this business, but you're buying a solid, no-debt operation that has been around for many years. Moreover, at $20 (over the counter) in mid-1987, it had the lowest McDep ratio of any production company in my coverage.

Wiser represents a good combined commodity play on natural gas and oil. Natural gas holdings (representing 53 percent of Wiser's property value) have a reserve-life index of fourteen years and include important properties on the Gulf Coast. Another asset is a portfolio of oil and gas securities, including Exxon at low cost. Of course, oil companies shouldn't have their money tied up in stock portfolios—investors should own those portfolios—so in a sense Wiser is too conservatively managed. Management could also afford to take on some debt to acquire producing properties and give stockholders more exposure to the upward trend in oil and gas values.

Wiser has been the subject of takeover interest from time to time, and I suspect somebody will eventually buy it out, paying a much higher price than we anticipate. I remember when Shell bought Belridge in 1979 for what seemed to be an astronomical price of $3.6 billion, or $9 a barrel in the ground for heavy oil reserves. At that time, one of my clients felt that Wiser might be "the Belridge of the East," since most of its oil reserves were in Appalachia, where there was a potential for enhanced recovery, much like the heavy oil in California. Appalachian oil lies close to the surface and, while the fields have all produced a considerable amount of oil over the years, there's still a lot left in the ground. Perhaps these reserves eventually will be recovered by Wiser and other companies such as Pennzoil and Marathon (a division of USX).

McDep helped lead me to Wiser late in 1986, when the stock was still priced near its July low of $14 and had the lowest McDep ratio (.73) of the ten largest production companies. I recommended the stock at that point, and a week later it caught a ride in the early-January rally by energy stocks, breaking out to a fifty-two-week high of $18 and eventually moving to $24 before settling back. Even at $15, Wiser remains a well-regarded company and a compelling value.

SOUTHWESTERN ENERGY

Stock price, 10/19/87: $25
McDep ratio: .80
Yield: 2.7 percent

Southwestern Energy, headquartered in Fayetteville, Arkansas, offers a choice, overlooked play on natural gas. Largely an oil and gas production company, it also owns a gas distribution system in Arkansas, so I include it in my pipeline group. Most significantly, 63 percent of the company's property value is represented by natural gas reserves with a reserve-life index of twenty years.

While on a marketing trip to Boston in October 1986, I told clients, "Prices for most pipeline stocks are still too high, but I'd be most comfortable owning Southwestern Energy, a quality little jewel with considerable long-life natural gas reserves. I don't think it will go up right away, but it ought to do nicely over time." Indeed, the stock improved only from $20 (with a McDep of .82) to $25 in mid-1987, where it had the second lowest McDep ratio (.90) of all the pipeline companies in my coverage.

A continued lack of investor recognition may mean that Southwestern Energy is still an intriguing, undervalued stock in view of its concentration on natural gas resources and positive industry trends. In addition to its low McDep ratio, Southwestern Energy has more sensitivity to changes in natural gas prices than any other pipeline company.

BURLINGTON NORTHERN

Stock price, 10/29/87: $57
McDep ratio: .78
Yield: 8.2 percent

When Boone Pickens was traveling about the country in September 1986 making a pitch for a new stock offering by his Mesa Limited Partnership, he was often asked what *he* would like to be buying. "Long-life gas reserves," he emphasized at one stop after another.

Mesa itself, Plains, and Dorchester Hugoton provide the choicest natural gas reserves, but if you also want to add a bit of diversity to your McDep Energy Fund, look into Burlington Northern. The largest U.S. railroad has become one of the biggest independent oil and gas producers by acquiring El Paso Company in 1983 and Southland Royalty Company in 1985. Most importantly, the company now has a valuable asset in long-life natural gas with a reserve-life index of seventeen years. Production is centered in the San Juan Basin, where there's potential to increase current reserves through additional drilling.

I'm confident about Burlington Northern's energy business and underlying energy values, but this represents just 30 percent of its property value. The other 70 percent includes the railroad, which appears to be a high-quality operation. If you're willing to bet that the railroad will fare reasonably well over the next couple of years, then a resurgent gas business should give the stock a healthy boost.

Periodic takeover rumors, usually involving Boone Pickens (who had a 2.4 percent stake the end of 1986), tend to bolster the stock temporarily, but invariably these rumors cool and the stock price settles a bit lower.

I include Burlington Northern in the group of diversified companies (page 209 in the Appendix), along with another well-regarded railroad, Union Pacific. The latter has some excellent gas production properties, especially in the Overthrust, but much less relative property value (13 percent versus 23 percent) in this area as compared to Burlington Northern. At $51 a share in mid-October, 1987, Union Pacific had a McDep only slightly higher than Burlington Northern (.81 to .78), but I would favor BN if you are choosing between the two stocks.

INTEGRATED OIL COMPANIES WITH SIGNIFICANT GAS RESERVES

Given my bullishness on natural gas prospects, I believe you should own not only at least one pure play producer but also an integrated oil company with an important percentage of property value represented by natural gas reserves. As the investment attractiveness of natural gas increases, pension fund managers and other institutional investors with billions of dollars to invest will be forced to buy this commodity through the high-cap integrated companies, as opposed to the much smaller independent producers.

Fortunately, a number of low-McDep companies happen to boast significant gas reserves and are the most sensitive to rising gas prices, as we can see in Table 4. Your attention should focus on the companies with the lowest ratio of market cap to gas reserves, since this indicates the greatest potential leverage. In other words, for a given increase in the value of natural gas reserves—assuming a proportional increase for everybody's gas holdings—the company with the lowest ratio will realize a greater percentage impact on its stock price.

Amoco, as I noted earlier in the book, is the standout gas play among the large integrated companies. It owns the most U.S. natural gas reserves and has a reserve-life index of sixteen years, comfortably above the industry average. Texaco, aided by its low McDep ratio, appears to be the second most attractive opportunity, especially in terms of its sensitivity to changes in natural gas prices. Meanwhile, Mobil's position as the country's third-largest owner of reserves should give its stock important leverage as the natural gas surplus disappears.

Unocal and Phillips are easily the best choices among the small integrateds.

You may wonder why I've largely avoided the natural gas pipeline companies in this chapter (with the exception of Southwestern Energy, which is two-thirds a production company). The reason, very simply, is that I would much rather buy and own the resource-rich companies. In fact, this preference for the production side of the oil and gas business—as opposed to refining, marketing, and distribution (i.e., the pipelines)—has been a consistent theme throughout the book, as reflected by the companies I'm recommending.

TABLE 5.1 U.S. OIL AND GAS INTEGRATED COMPANIES' SENSITIVITY TO NATURAL GAS

	PRICE 10/19 1987 ($/SH)	SHARES (MM)	MARKET CAP ($MM)	U.S. NATURAL GAS (BCF)	MARKET CAP/ NATURAL GAS
Small					
Quaker State	15	26	400	77	5.2
Murphy	29	34	1,000	223	4.5
Total (North America)	15	24	360	84	4.3
American Petrofina	64	13	840	239	3.5
Pennzoil	51	48	2,500	883	2.8
Kerr-McGee	36	48	1,700	616	2.8
Amerada Hess	23	89	2,100	822	2.6
Crown Central (low vote rights)	16	9	140	79	1.8
Sun	36	108	3,900	2,377	1.6
Phillips	12	230	2,700	3,232	.8
Unocal	29	116	3,300	4,500	.7
Composite			19,000	13,100	1.5
Large					
British Petroleum	60	460	27,700	1,513	18
Royal Dutch/Shell	95	450	43,000	6,400	6.7
Exxon	34	1,440	48,000	10,380	4.6
Atlantic Richfield	65	180	11,700	5,923	2
Chevron	41	340	14,000	7,509	1.9
Texaco	33	270	8,800	5,132	1.7
USX	22	270	5,800	3,436	1.7
Mobil	32	410	13,200	7,855	1.7
Amoco	60	260	15,600	10,270	1.5
Composite			188,000	58,000	3.2

In my estimation, production represents far greater value, now and in the future. Resources, as we've seen, are not reproducible; you can build another pipeline without much trouble, but natural gas is only located in certain natural accumulations, and there don't appear to be any more Hugoton or San Juan-type fields left to discover in the United States. Thus, increases in the value of this resource are going to accrue far more to the holder of the resource (the producer) than to the transporting pipeline company. Gas pipeline companies are middlemen, like the refiners in oil, and their profit is a much smaller percentage of the delivered price than the producer's profit. I prefer to invest in the producer's upside potential.

CHAPTER 6

TRUSTS AND PARTNERSHIPS— HIGH YIELDS AND PURE PLAYS

Royalty trusts and master limited partnerships (now numbering over twenty in my McDep coverage) offer several attractive candidates that can help balance your energy portfolio. Most of them provide high cash payouts that are largely tax sheltered (representing an average yield of about 10 percent in 1986), and they offer a pure play investment in the production of U.S. oil and gas reserves. At the same time, the stronger trusts and partnerships tend to be fully priced as measured by McDep, indicating modest capital gains potential, especially in comparison to lower yielding, lower McDep production companies and integrated oils. You must decide how important current yield is to your overall portfolio, while taking into account an entity's total yearly return (stock price appreciation plus dividends). This chapter will help you ferret out the soundest opportunities.

THE VIRTUES FOR INVESTORS

Trusts and partnerships trade exactly like stocks (mostly on the New York Stock Exchange), except that the "shares" you buy are known as units. Let's review their attractions, then explore the caveats.

1. *High taxable-equivalent yields for investors.* Since trusts and partnerships do not pay corporate taxes, there's much more cash flow left over to pay out as dividends. Moreover, much of that cash flow is sheltered by a combination of intangible drilling costs, cost depletion, and other factors, thereby reducing taxable income for the investor. A 10 percent cash yield thus represents an even higher taxable-equivalent yield.

Tax regulations require trusts to pay out more than 90 percent of their cash flow after drilling expenditures. Some trusts pay these dividends monthly, but the payout can fluctuate through the year, reflecting seasonal demand for oil and gas. Dividend payouts by partnerships are discretionary, but most of them are paid quarterly.

Shareholders like the income stream coupled with tax savings on that income. That financial sentiment helps provide a floor of support for the stock price of well-regarded trusts and partnerships; if the price declines a bit, the resulting yield goes up and becomes even more attractive, especially to investors who are confident about the long-term trend for oil and gas prices.

2. *High dividend payouts give investors control over*

reinvestment of cash flow and help discipline management. Since unit holders (shareholders) receive nearly all the cash flow from trusts and partnerships, you can make your own reinvestment decision with that money; you're not reliant on the management of an integrated oil company that might be reinvesting excess cash flow in areas you're not too excited about, such as refining/marketing and nonenergy areas.

Meanwhile, since stock prices for most trusts and partnerships are strongly supported by the prospect of a high and sustainable dividend payout, the pressure to meet this payout provides an important form of management accountability. In order to maintain a competitive payout, management must raise new funds from lenders and investors to expand current production and sustain cash flow. That is beneficial because the discipline of the capital markets is impartial; if management's spending plans are not deemed worthy, lenders won't lend and investors won't buy a new offering. A management that must depend on a broad spectrum of investors like this will have a difficult time getting support for its project unless the need is convincing.

3. *Trusts and partnerships are concentrated on a single function—exploration and production in U.S. oil and gas fields.* This means that investors can better determine value, since management is focused on that one responsibility and is not being diverted by forays into unfamiliar areas of the business or other areas of the economy. Nor are there oil refineries or troubled steel mills or production facilities in unstable foreign countries to cause alarm.

THE POTENTIAL PITFALLS

When oil prices were plunging in January 1986, I was quoted in a *Wall Street Journal* story about trusts and partnerships, warning about the potential risks that I felt lay ahead. After reading the story, my wife, Louise, said, "I thought you *liked* trusts and partnerships." That was true, and I still recommend a number of them, but I also like to point out the downside risk in any investment. So if you want to add one of these entities to your portfolio, here are some considerations to keep in mind.

First, the higher the McDep ratio, the more you must trust management's ability to do a superior job in the future. Up to a 1.0 McDep, you're basically buying oil and gas reserves in the ground, since 1.0 represents the theoretical present value of these properties—what companies would pay (and are paying) in the open market. A McDep higher than 1.0 means that you're relying on management to earn this premium by the way it manages existing properties and adds to reserves.

Basically, unless you're buying a management like Boone Pickens at Mesa Limited Partnership or reserves in high-quality gas fields such as the Hugoton or San Juan Basin, I think that McDeps higher than about 1.25 represent too high a premium to pay.

Second, when you buy a premium McDep entity, you should have reasonable confidence in the oil and gas price trend. Since trusts and partnerships represent a pure way to play the energy production business, a high-McDep entity doesn't have as much cushion in its stock price for a decline in prices, as that stock price has been reflecting an optimistic outlook. (Still, even in 1986, the large trusts and partnerships with manageable debt held up quite well, supported by their dividend yields and rebounding industry prospects. At year's end they were still the best-regarded structures for holding oil and gas reserves, almost all of them selling at a premium to what their properties were worth.)

Third, since the cash payout (and more specifically, the taxable equivalent yield) is underpinning the market price for many trusts and partnerships, you should always try to determine how secure the dividend is. High yields are alluring, but only if the payout is supported by the fundamentals of the underlying properties. This is especially important at the high-McDep companies, where the dividend could be artificially high—propped up by management—and thus could be supporting an unrealistically high stock price.

A good example here would be Diamond Shamrock Offshore Partners, an unusually high-McDep (1.40) partnership whose stock price ($17) and dividend yield (16 percent) have been artificially supported by a corporate parent who has "guaranteed" a $2.80-a-year distribution through 1989. Although Diamond Shamrock (now Maxus Energy) maintained this dividend all through 1986 and into mid-1987, I warned my clients that dividend guarantees aren't legal commitments and they serve to keep the stock price propped up. Moreover, if control of Maxus Energy were to change, the new buyer could terminate the partnership, and thus the dividend guarantee. The value of the partnership then would reflect the value of underlying properties, or about $12 a unit based on a McDep ratio of 1.0. The partnership's gas properties also have a short reserve-life index of just six years. While it appears the dividend will indeed be paid through 1989, investors are putting more reliance on that dividend than they probably should for a short-life partnership.

Another potential danger can be a dividend that is being supported at an "assured" level by a struggling parent company. In 1986, for example, the weakening financial condition of Enserch, a pipeline operation, was threatening the pledged $2.40-a-year dividend at Enserch Exploration Partners and was helping to undermine the partnership's stock price. Even though the partnership had choice long-life gas properties and a low debt-to-property ratio, it was a captive of the parent's financial health. In fact, management had to cut the partnership's payout to $1.20 for 1987 (still an 11 percent yield on a $11 stock, with a McDep of .84).

Fourth, keep an eye on debt, though this is much less a concern with the worst conditions behind us and energy prices rising. In fact, nearly all trusts and partnerships have comfortably low levels of debt, except for Damson Energy with a debt-to-property ratio of .67. Yet in a strengthening industry environment, that debt can actually provide Damson with good financial leverage, similar to what I anticipate with Consolidated Oil and Gas (page 139). I'll discuss Damson's high-risk appeal later in this chapter.

PROMISING ROYALTY TRUSTS

Boone Pickens launched the royalty trust theme in 1979 when he created Mesa Royalty Trust, followed in 1982 by Mesa Offshore Trust. Although we're not likely to see many new trusts formed under the latest tax law (since certain changes chilled their appeal as a restructuring device for big companies), we can still pick from several good investment choices.

My two favorites are underscored by long-life oil and gas reserves, since these assets will last well into the future and will increase in value as energy prices reach higher levels. Higher prices also will inspire volume growth by these producers and will provide greater cash flow, which should translate to stock appreciation and higher dividend payouts.

SAN JUAN BASIN ROYALTY TRUST

Stock price, 10/19/87: $8.6
McDep ratio: 1.03
Dividend yield: 4.4 percent

This is a high-quality operation that has held up well over the years, at a time when many production companies have gone out of business. Burlington Northern operates the properties, having acquired the trust through its purchase of Southland Royalty in 1985.

Although San Juan's yield is only 4.5 percent (half of it tax free), many investors regard the trust as an energy bond that offers relative long-term safety and a stable income stream that should escalate over time. Virtually all the property value is represented by natural gas production and reserves in the San Juan Basin of northwest New Mexico. The reserve-life index is twenty-six years, making investors willing to accept a lower dividend return in view of the trust's long-term potential.

As a royalty trust, San Juan pays out all of its cash flow from current production to investors. This production was down a bit through most of 1987, but the San Juan Basin is an area that can come back—and we will be needing more natural gas in this country, even while paying increasingly higher prices. Thus cash flow could easily be several times higher, benefiting the stock price and dividend payout.

In a sense, San Juan Basin is a low-priced Plains Petroleum with a dividend. Both of them are concentrated on choice, long-life gas reserves, have no debt, and can easily meet increased production opportunities.

One other attraction of San Juan Basin for certain investors would be the fact that it generates positive taxable income as a trust. This income might be used to offset passive income from other tax shelters. Trust income may also be useful for investors who have taxable losses going unused.

PERMIAN BASIN ROYALTY TRUST

Stock price, 10/19/87: $6.3
McDep ratio: .97
Dividend yield: 7 percent

The main attraction here is relatively long-life oil production in the Permian Basin of West Texas, including part of the famed Yates field (the cornerstone of USX's oil reserves). Oil represents 70 percent of Permian's property value and has an above-average reserve-life index of twelve years, which I feel is understated, since engineers were compelled to use depressed prices at year-end 1986 in their calculations.

Permian offers one of the relatively few pure plays in high-quality oil reserves. And as the old saying goes, "The market always pays higher for a pure play." Yet while these oil reserves can help justify an investment at these price levels, keep in mind that Permian's present value of equity is only $9 under my projected 1990 valuations, when the going value of oil in the ground equals its historic high.

PARTNERSHIPS WITH ATTRACTIVE PROSPECTS

Although certain provisions in the 1986 tax law will curb the rapid increase in limited partnerships, I still track fourteen of them with my McDep coverage. The potential "buy" list narrows considerably, however, when we screen out partnerships with unrealistically high McDep ratios and unexciting oil and gas reserves.

I've already detailed my favorite small partnership, Dorchester Hugoton (page 135), while Mesa Limited Partnership, which I'll soon discuss, remains my clear-cut choice among the larger entities. Two other possibilities could be:

1. Damson Energy—which subdivides into Damson Energy A and Damson Energy B—but only on the assumption that it has survived bankruptcy and may now have clear sailing ahead in a strengthening energy business. If you have an adventurous spirit, look into Damson as a low-priced ($1), low-McDep (.83) stock with surprisingly ample natural gas reserves in relation to its market cap. The partnership also has the lowest ratio of stock price to present value of equity of any trust or partnership in my McDep coverage, and would theoretically more than

quadruple (to about $5½) with a return to historic highs in oil and gas values.

More than a few investors will shudder at the memory of how much Damson Energy's stock plummeted in 1986 and well into 1987, which should serve notice of the risk in betting on Damson's recovery. Nevertheless, what goes down fast and survives can sometimes come back. If Damson Energy can continue to lower its unusually high administrative costs (which currently penalize my valuation of their natural gas reserves by about $.40 an mcf) and survive two lawsuits, then it could eventually reward the speculating investor.

(Another low-priced, low-McDep stock among the trusts and partnerships is Apache Petroleum [$5.6 a share and a McDep of .91], but I would avoid this partnership. Although predominantly a gas producer, Apache's reserve-life index of only five years increases the investment risk and limits potential. In my eyes, the best characteristic for a partnership is to have long-life reserves beyond the average of eleven years.)

2. A well-positioned partnership is Sun Energy Partners ($16 a share and a McDep of .84), which represents all of the Sun Company's U.S. exploration and production activities. Two-thirds of the partnership's property value is represented by domestic oil reserves (an industry average reserve-life index of nine years), which are four times greater than the next largest partnership, Union Exploration Partners.

MESA LIMITED PARTNERSHIP

Stock price, 10/19/87: $13
McDep ratio: .89
Dividend yield: 16 percent

With T. Boone Pickens at the helm, a rich dividend, and superb long-life gas reserves (eighteen years), Mesa is clearly a compelling investment. Some investors were scared away by Mesa's premium McDep ratio of 1.30 in late 1986, worried that there was little upside potential in such a fully valued stock. Yet when I raised my property value estimates in early 1987, Mesa's McDep dropped accordingly—but certainly not its future potential.

A number of important factors make me confident about Mesa's total return to shareholders (dividends plus stock appreciation) in the coming years.

1. *The Boone Pickens factor.* Boone is sometimes criticized for embodying what he finds endemic at certain large oil companies—that is, managers who are too deeply entrenched and paid too much. Boone himself is indeed entrenched and well paid, but there's a crucial difference: He performs. He makes money for his stockholders.

Mesa's total return from 1976 to 1986 (counting dividends and the value of various distributions such as two royalty trusts) was 19 percent a year. The average integrated company returned 11 percent. Moreover, as general partner and owner of 7 percent of Mesa's units outstanding, Boone is not simply responsible for the partnership's efficient operation, but has a personal stake in Mesa's future stock market performance. I like to invest in a manager who senses that kind of shareholder pressure.

I should point out that my firm, Donaldson, Lufkin and Jenrette, has helped Mesa since about 1969 and has provided investment banking services from time to time. However, Boone and I have established our relationship on a research basis and we've become good friends. We get together occasionally and we stay in touch through my monthly publication, *Oil and Gas Valuation*, which updates my thoughts about the oil and gas business. Through our conversations and my research reports, he's already familiar with my opinions about a specific company he may be pursuing as a takeover target. A good example occurred in September 1983, when I was in Alaska on a business trip and I heard that Boone had made his first bid for KN Energy. I called him up to confirm what was happening and he said, "That was your number one choice, wasn't it?" Indeed, KN Energy was my strongest recommendation at the time in the natural gas group.

I'm the first to admit that Boone has certainly helped my career along by promoting, hastening, and implementing the restructuring theme I've been advocating since 1981. But his strategy of seeking out unrecognized values in the integrated oil group, reflecting my research emphasis, could become crucial to Mesa's sustained success as a partnership (as I'll explain in the next section). Fortunately for Mesa, and Mesa shareholders, Boone is in a class by himself in terms of doing oil deals.

Another characteristic I like about Boone is that he's an innovative thinker who doesn't rest on his laurels. He's right on top of what's going on in the industry, coping with the tough times and capitalizing on improving trends. Boone has been particularly astute in anticipating changes in the industry and adjusting to its fluctuating fortunes. For example, he showed how the limited partnership form can serve different purposes by converting his whole company into a partnership in late 1985, with the largest publicly held capitalization of all the energy partnerships. At about the same time, shortly before oil prices finally cracked and plummeted toward $10 a barrel, Pickens protected Mesa's 1986 oil production by hedging on the oil futures market. While several other companies were building up inventories, he *sold* more than 3 million barrels worth of futures contracts at $26.50 per barrel. That was roughly equivalent to the amount of oil Mesa projected to produce in 1986. So Boone was protected, no matter how low oil might have gone that year, knowing that he had already "sold" his oil at $26.50 a barrel. He covered a bit too early—at $15—but the overall strategy certainly paid off as he pocketed for his unit holders an $11-a-barrel difference on a whole year's crude-oil volume.

Meanwhile, with Mesa's debt-to-property ratio at an unsafe .46 in early 1986, and oil prices in a free-fall, Boone correctly perceived the dangers and began scaling back on Mesa's debt. The key move was his acquisition of Pioneer Corporation, a low-debt company that he bought with Mesa equity, helping to sharply lower his partnership's debt ratio to an eventual .11.

2. *Long-life gas reserves.* Boone Pickens is so closely identified with the takeover movement that investors tend to overlook the fact that Mesa is the largest independent gas producer in the United States.

Strengthened by the Pioneer acquisition—which raised reserves from 1.3 trillion cubic feet (tcf) to 2.025 tcf—natural gas now represents 79 percent of Mesa's property value, with two-thirds of the reserves in the Hugoton fields of Kansas and Texas. These Hugoton reserves give Mesa's gas an overall reserve-life index of eighteen years, and will allow the partnership to capitalize on positive cycles in the industry for years to come.

For example, Mesa's Hugoton reserves are flowing at far below their potential, but additional drilling in the Kansas Hugoton—started in early 1987 and extending over a four-year span—will increase future production capacity as demand and prices move higher. This eventually will increase cash flow by a significant amount and will broaden proven reserves. In fact, a quarter of Mesa's total current production is sold at just $.28/mcf under a contract expiring in December 1989. After that, the gas can be sold at much higher market prices.

3. *A dividend yield of 16 percent.* Mesa's stock is obviously supported by its $2-a-year payout, most of which is tax free. Boone has assured investors that the dividend can be paid well into 1988—and beyond. There are no guarantees, of course, given the near-term challenges facing Mesa as Boone tries to pursue deals (i.e., takeover attempts) that are necessary to maintain the partnership's reserves and cash flow—and thus the high payout. However, even if the dividend can't be covered by current cash flow, I'm confident it will still be paid. Mesa has low debt and hardly any bank debt, which means

there aren't any lenders that will restrict Mesa from making that payment. I'm projecting that Mesa's cash flow will be able to exceed dividend distributions in 1988, assuming only a modest increase in oil and gas prices. Also remember that this dividend risk is well publicized and therefore already reflected in the stock price. In addition, there's always the possibility that Mesa's payout may even increase over the next few years if circumstances fall into place.

4. *Growth by acquisition.* Since Mesa's reserves are fully valued in the stock market, Boone Pickens must acquire other oil and gas properties in order to give Mesa's stock greater appreciation potential.

Coming out of tough times in the oil business, Mesa can grow somewhat by acquiring small- to medium-sized properties in the $100 million range (one example being its equity investment of about $80 million in NRM Energy Company, a low-priced limited partnership, in November 1986). Realistically, however, Mesa needs to pull off a major deal that turns one invested dollar into two or three. This means pursuing and hopefully acquiring a low-McDep integrated company like Texaco or Mobil, then bringing out the underlying values through appropriate restructuring. An acquisition of this magnitude could double Mesa's stock price while enriching shareholders at the targeted company. The opportunities are certainly out there and Boone has a healthy war chest, especially after his active investing in two defense companies and Newmont Mining during the summer of 1987. Perhaps these forays outside the oil and gas business were designed to throw his eventual targets off guard. Invest in Mesa and you can share in some of that excitement down the road.

THE MESA PREFERRED ISSUE

Stock price, 10/19/87: $10
McDep ratio: .89
Yield: 13 percent

The Mesa Limited Partnership preferred A stock was created in June 1986 as part of the Pioneer acquisition. The preference feature—guaranteeing that the $1.50-a-year dividend will be paid before the common dividend until 1991—may prove meaningless if oil and gas prices continue to rise and Mesa's cash flow remains strong. In fact, the more optimistic you are about the energy rebound and Boone's ability to make significant acquisitions, the more you should favor Mesa common, rather than the preferred. If these positive events unfold, Mesa's common dividend ($2 a year) will be safe—and could increase—while the preferred dividend has been specifically locked in at $1.50 a year. Also, the preferred reverts into common units in 1991.

CHAPTER 7

TAKING ACTION

Now that you're familiar with my favorite oil and gas stocks and the energy outlook that gives them such promise, it's time to start making money.

This chapter will draw largely on my own rewarding experiences as a stock picker and investor. A $10,000 investment in my published recommendations starting in mid-1977 and redeployed as recommendations changed would have been worth about $140,000 in mid-1987, for a total return of about 30 percent a year. While historical performance doesn't guarantee future results, I'm confident my strategy can continue to pay off in the years ahead. Also keep in mind that I'm emphasizing the philosophy and guidelines that tend to influence my particular buy and sell decisions. This personal investment style may conflict with your own investment approach, but my experience has been that clients tend to feel comfortable with a strategy that makes them money.

ASSET ALLOCATION

Whether you are starting from scratch or already own several oil and gas stocks in an existing brokerage account, think about constructing a self-managed McDep Energy Fund. This will help focus your attention on the oil and gas industry while giving your overall investment portfolio a clearly defined area of diversification. Tracking your fund's progress from week to week and quarter to quarter can also be fun—and instructive.

Using either regular investment funds or existing IRA/ Keogh money, it's easy to establish a self-directed account through a bank or brokerage house, even if you only intend to buy fifty shares of one or two companies in the beginning. A self-directed account will allow you to make your own buy and sell decisions, drawing on the advice in this book and your own instincts. Although a broker can prove helpful, alerting you to recent company developments you may have missed that could affect its stock performance, ultimately you must be faithful to your convictions—and not be easily swayed by a broker's contrary opinion. Remember, many of my recommended stocks tend to be overlooked, unappreciated, or unloved by other analysts, but often that's exactly why you want to be buying them, given the criteria I've established.

Before taking action, try to determine just how much money you want to have invested in oil and gas stocks six months from now. Then plan to invest that amount gradually rather than all at once.

Let's say, for instance, that you want to commit $10,000 to energy stocks from the accumulated cash in your IRA account. If the typical stock is about $30, then we're talking about buying one hundred shares of three stocks as an initial six-month goal. Later, you may want to add to these positions or buy new stocks as funds become available through your yearly IRA contributions, accumulated dividends, and capital gains.

The key attitude starting out is that you're going to accumulate stock over a period of time—not all today. I remember back in the 1960s, several years after my wife's father had died, she kept encouraging her mother to invest some of his estate in the stock market. Finally, early in 1967, her skeptical mother and an equally stubborn lawyer went out and hired an investment firm that proceeded to invest the entire portfolio in the stock market—in one day! The investment counselor also succeeded in catching a multiyear peak in the market. I have subsequently heard Louise advise friends many times over the years, "Never invest all at once." I think that's sound advice, whatever amount you're going to put into the stock market. By exercising some restraint as you commit your capital, you can take advantage of short-term declines to pay a cheaper price for a company you've been following. And, if the energy sector keeps moving up from the day you make your first purchase, you'll already have a winner or two in your McDep Fund as you use the McDep technique to identify the inevitable laggards that can still represent relative bargains.

Obviously, the money you invest in energy stocks should be kept in perspective to your overall portfolio. As bullish as you might be about long-term prospects for oil and gas stocks, you shouldn't risk having most all of your money in just one sector of the economy. If your timing is impeccable, betting on this sector could make you feel like an investment genius, but that's taking an unreasonable gamble with your money.

My many years of experience in the energy business

have taught me how important it is to have my investments spread out so that I can help insure a strong overall total return from one year to the next with *all* my invested money. My own energy portfolio, for example, rose 79 percent in 1979 and 97 percent in 1980, only to drop 12 percent in 1981 and 14 percent in 1982, before rebounding upward by 70 percent in 1983. Therefore, I keep my money invested in three areas: (1) energy-related stocks, (2) cash, via money-market funds, and (3) a self-directed fund invested in nonenergy stocks. This gives my portfolio the balance and diversity to keep growing every year, taking into account the often conflicting trends in the stock market and the economy. I had an excellent year in 1987 as my nonenergy stocks benefitted from a continuing era of low growth and low inflation, yet meanwhile I had my ongoing position in oil and gas stocks that would provide a hedge against any return to inflationary times.

While a McDep Energy Fund will help diversify your overall investment portfolio, make sure you also stay diversified within the fund. At a minimum, plan to buy at least one integrated oil company with a high percentage of U.S. oil and gas reserves and one natural gas producer so that you can participate in the upward trend in both areas. Then, if you have an interest in building up cash with a high dividend payout, add a high-yielding trust or partnership. Beyond that, add the integrated company with the lowest McDep ratio in its group as a way to possibly profit from the restructuring/takeover theme. This combination will give you capital gains potential, quarterly dividend returns, and portfolio representation in the two most important segments of the energy business—oil production and natural gas production. (Rather than relying on high-yielding stocks as a way to build reinvestment funds, I'd rather focus on stocks with terrific capital gains potential and then eventually sell off some or all of the shares to build cash.)

Another important reminder here is that you shouldn't let any one stock dominate your portfolio. I'm a pretty conservative investor and no matter how excited I might get about a particular stock, I try to limit how many shares I'll own of that stock (or total amount of money invested). I'll bend my rules and double up when I'm absolutely convinced the payoff is going to be there—as I did with Supron and Marathon—but generally I prefer to establish my desired positions with one or two purchases, then sit and wait for the eventual payoff.

INVESTING THROUGH AN IRA/KEOGH ACCOUNT

Like millions of other Americans, you may have an IRA or Keogh retirement account that has grown well past $10,000 in value, but is being underutilized as an advantageous vehicle for investing in the stock market. This is particularly true if you simply have your funds parked in CDs and money-market accounts that are currently paying relatively low interest rates at a time when you should become a more aggressive investor.

If this is your situation, I'd recommend opening a self-directed IRA/Keogh account so that you can start investing in oil and gas stocks and give your money much greater upside appreciation potential in these days of single-digit interest rates.

Although there's no perfect vehicle for your McDep Energy Fund, IRA/Keogh accounts certainly offer an attractive investment environment. Consider these benefits:

- Since all income is now taxed at the same rate (capital gains, dividends, and interest), an IRA/Keogh shelters your investment and thus allows you to have long-term, tax-deferred growth. Dividends and capital gains (profits) earned from your investments are exempt from tax until the funds are withdrawn, starting when you are age fifty-nine and a half. This means that your earnings will continue to appreciate and compound over the years and therefore multiply much faster than if taxes had been paid on such earnings as you went along. The fact that you can reinvest the government's tax money in this manner means that you will be able to accumulate more funds for continued reinvestment as you postpone paying taxes on your earnings.

- As dividend payouts continue to grow at most of the integrated companies, after stagnating, declining, or even disappearing in 1986–87, this taxable income can be reinvested and won't increase your tax bill every year as you build your fund's overall value. This also means that trusts and partnerships that have high but largely tax-exempt payouts should be held in a regular stock account. Otherwise you're wasting the tax-exempt advantage of these invested funds.

- Ideally, an IRA/Keogh account should encourage you to take a long-term perspective with your stocks as you wait for a significant profit to eventually unfold at a Dorchester Hugoton or a Unocal. Knowing that your money is, in effect, locked away for many years and not easily or cheaply withdrawn to pay for college tuition or a new house should help you stay the course.

On the other hand, IRA/Keoghs can also be viewed as ideal trading accounts, since the profits on short-term trades are tax-deferred. The drawback is that you can eat up a lot of potential profits with frequent brokerage transactions. Moreover, any stock losses inside an IRA/Keogh, should they occur, can't be written off against stock gains. I trust this book can spare you from these losers.

STOCK SELECTION

Once you have established an overall strategy for your McDep Energy Fund and the appropriate brokerage account, it's time to take action on my recommended stocks while searching for new buying opportunities.

UPDATING MCDEP

The first important step is to determine, "Where are we?" This means calculating where oil prices, individual stock prices, and McDep ratios stand today in relation to those I've quoted in the book.

This may seem statistically intimidating, but you'll find that it's easy to do. First find the stock market listings in today's newspaper and then turn to my tables in the Appendix (beginning on page 195), where I supply a line of pertinent data for all one hundred of the companies I track with my McDep analysis. There are two sets of calculations here.

One set is based on oil and natural gas valued at $8 a barrel and $1.10/mcf in the ground (as opposed to what they sell for on the open market). These were the prevailing values for oil and gas as of August 28, 1987, when crude-oil futures were about $20 a barrel. By using the figures I've provided, you can recalculate the McDep ratios for companies I've recommended and those that may have a particular appeal. Multiply the stock price times shares outstanding to find a company's market capitalization, then add long-term debt to obtain the numerator (the top number in the McDep calculations). Assume that property value has remained unchanged as the denominator, and divide that number into the numerator to obtain a current McDep ratio. Ideally, you should update McDeps for all the stocks in a particular grouping so that you can judge relative values and begin isolating the most promising low-McDep candidates.

A more important set of calculations is based on oil and gas at $12/bbl and $1.50/mcf in the ground. These values represent the historic highs of 1980–81, which is where I believe we're headed, perhaps in 1990. By calculating McDep ratios based on these target values, you can begin to spotlight those companies with the greatest stock market appreciation potential over the next several years as we build toward a new cyclical high.

Once you've determined the necessary McDep ratios, compare a company's current stock price to my present value of equity (or "breakup value," as represented by a McDep of 1.0), which I've given for each stock in the appendix tables. Again, I've calculated present value of equity based on oil in the ground at both $8 and $12 so that you can judge a stock's theoretical appreciation potential over the near term and a few years out. This should lend some excitement of anticipation for what lies ahead at a number of oil and gas companies.

UPDATING COMPANY DEVELOPMENTS

Next, it's time to update recent developments at the companies spotlighted by McDep analysis, in relation to what I've written about a particular company in this book. This search should uncover any restructuring steps, changes in corporate control, stock splits, dividend increases, earnings reports, and major new oil and gas discoveries that have had an impact on the company's stock performance in recent months and could be affecting its near-term prospects. Here's the kind of homework you ought to consider doing:

- Write or call the companies that interest you and ask for their current annual report and the latest quarterly report. Many investors tend to ignore the company itself as a source of information, but these reports will certainly help you update recent developments and tell you a bit about management's future outlook and professed goals with the corporation or partnership.
- Review back issues of *Value Line* (available at most public libraries) for information about the oil and gas stocks tracked by that publication. Each company is updated every quarter, and important developments during the interim are referenced in the weekly index. You can rely on *Value Line*'s statistical information (though it lacks the most important aspect of my work—the present value of oil and gas reserves), but be wary of their famous "timeliness" ratings for energy stocks; they emphasize earnings momentum and current cash flow, whereas I stress underlying value and cash flow beyond the next quarter. Basically, I would turn to them for information, not investment advice.

174

- If you have computer and subscription access, turn to the Dow Jones News Retrieval Service, CompuServe, and other computer-based electronic retrieval sources. Realistically, that's the best way to become updated on a company, by doing a headline search for news relating to that company for the past three months or so. However, charges can run up quickly, so know what you want before you go on line.

- Finally, ask your broker for pertinent company research reports (e.g., an existing "buy" recommendation) and industry updates by the firm's specialists. If you're paying full commission dollars, try to get your money's worth, but always remember that you're reading the work of an analyst who may have an entirely different perspective and bias concerning the oil and gas business and specific stocks within that universe. He or she could thus unwittingly lead you away from the very stocks I'd like to see you buy.

LAUNCHING YOUR FUND

"Here lies Lester Bigelow," read the tombstone in a *New Yorker* cartoon. "He bought high and sold low." This investment fate is an understandable fear, and I don't mean to dismiss the importance of caution as you narrow your selection of stocks and try to sense which ones to buy for your energy fund—and at what price. Like many investors, you may feel more comfortable delaying your initial purchases until you've had a chance to study relative stock performances for a week or two, hoping to acquire a promising stock at a lower price.

The danger in this approach, however, is that analysis can give you paralysis and keep you on the sidelines too long. Nobody I know has been able to master timing in the stock market, so when it comes time to launch your McDep Energy Fund, don't hesitate too long at getting your feet wet. After narrowing your search to perhaps four or five stocks, buy the one that appears to be the most under-valued—ideally, the integrated company or producer with the lowest McDep ratio based on my $12/$1.50 tables, using current stock prices. Don't worry that you may be paying too high a price, for what counts is that you start building a position in the oil and gas sector. The direct financial involvement will help make you a better investor by sharpening your focus on this area of the economy and the stocks represented here.

Another reason I like to step in and buy a new stock I like, with minimal worry about the price I'm paying (pro-viding the McDep ratio is relatively low), is the realization that I can't expect to time successfully either the stock market or the oil market. Good entry points are rarely obvious until one can look back with perfect hindsight. But if you have a long-term perspective when you buy low-McDep stocks, "paying up" a bit in price is not going to have any important effect on your eventual payoff; what counts is that you weren't afraid to wade in and buy that stock when it was, in retrospect, cheaply priced.

If energy stocks as a group have been relatively quiet in recent weeks as you read this book, or perhaps are even trending downward after a strong performance in 1987, one investment danger will be that you try to hold back until it appears these stocks are ready to roll again. While it may seem prudent to continue studying the market and prospective energy stocks, my bet is that you'll hesitate too long when these stocks suddenly bolt higher. You'll wait to confirm that this is indeed a new bull move and not a short-lived upward "spike," but once this conviction sets in—that oil prices are indeed moving to a higher level, perhaps reflecting heightened tensions in the Middle East— you'll either end up chasing the stocks you like by paying considerably higher prices, or you'll continue watching in frustration as a window of opportunity closes.

So as you put my book to work, establish a base position in two or three promising stocks, knowing that you may be able to capitalize on future price weaknesses by buying more shares at lower prices, thus lowering your overall cost basis. This approach will get some of your money invested in energy stocks and working on your behalf as they move higher over time. Ultimately, you'll be a less frustrated and more confident investor as you build a successful energy portfolio.

TIMING FACTORS WHEN YOU'RE BUYING

Once you've made the first purchase for your energy fund, keep these timing factors in mind as you try to add to your existing positions at opportune times while seeking out new buying opportunities among the stocks you are following:

1. *If you like a stock's fundamentals but you're wary about its current price and the industry's near-term outlook, hedge your commitment by buying just half of your intended position.*

If the stock proceeds to decline but seems to

177

find "support" near a certain price, follow your original conviction and try to complete your position. Conversely, when a stock moves up strongly after your initial purchase and is no longer a low-McDep stock in its group, be happy that you bought when you did, but resist adding to your position. Instead, focus on those stocks that are more attractively priced within the McDep framework.

For example, in late December 1986 I encouraged clients to establish half a position in Wiser Oil (page 142), not knowing for sure if oil stocks were going to continue moving up or suddenly weaken if the recent OPEC accord failed to support crude oil prices above $18. I was confident, though, that Wiser was a long-term bargain at $14 (near its fifty-two-week low). The stock subsequently advanced 30 percent in January (to $18) and I decided to delay filling out my position, sensing there could be traditional spring weakness in the oil markets. Wiser proceeded to hit $24, but by mid-1987 had settled back at $20, where it had the lowest McDep ratio (.78) among the sixteen stocks in my grouping of U.S. oil and gas production companies.

2. *When energy stocks have had a strong recent run, use McDep as a tool to help you do some bargain hunting.*

Invariably, several low-McDep companies will have underperformed during this stretch and may now represent excellent bargains—especially as other investors begin to isolate and recognize these laggards. Instead of chasing stocks that have been rising strongly without any notable price correction and are now near the top of their group as ranked by McDep ratios, look for those stocks in the same group that haven't moved much in recent weeks or months. Even if these lower McDep stocks continue to muddle along, you likely will be paying a bargain price over time as the value in these stocks is eventually brought out or realized.

This advice reflects the fact that I'm a value investor as opposed to one who likes to bet on momentum. That is, I'm more likely to buy an undervalued stock that has had poor recent momentum in terms of price behavior and volume than a "hot" stock with strong momentum. To me, the implication is that there's more relative value left to come out in a lower McDep company.

3. *Be confident about stepping in and buying when near-term factors send stock prices dropping in the opposite direction of long-term values.*

There will be inevitable slumps in oil prices and isolated corporate setbacks as we work our way toward the next cyclical peak in the energy business, but you should be ready to capitalize on the resulting stock corrections and regard them as opportunities to accumulate more shares of the stocks you already own, or finally to buy stocks you have been following for perhaps many months, waiting for the price pullback that usually comes with patience.

Adverse developments are obviously disappointing, since we all like to see our investment ideas pay off as soon as possible, but these setbacks can also help you build an energy portfolio at reasonable prices—providing you have the conviction to ride out my convictions about the stocks featured in this book.

An example of this philosophy came in November 1984, when long-anticipated hearings about infill drilling in the Kansas Hugoton gas field were delayed indefinitely. This caused a fairly significant correction in two of my recommended stocks, KN Energy and Dorchester Hugoton, which stood to benefit considerably from infill drilling. Still convinced that the issue would eventually be favorably resolved, I encouraged my clients to regard the setback as "an opportunity for the future," noting that the prices of both stocks were at their year-earlier level. "The attraction in these two stocks is just as good as a year ago." Indeed, as we saw in the natural gas chapter, both stocks proceeded to reward investors with strong gains once the hearings were finally held and infill drilling was approved in 1986.

Many of my clients also took advantage of a sudden, unexpected long-term bargain price for Texaco stock when the company was rocked by a $10 billion judgment in the lawsuit brought about by Pennzoil. The news sliced more than 10 points off Texaco stock in late 1985, allowing investors to establish major positions between $26 and $30. Texaco eventually worked its way up to about $40, only to offer investors another bite at the apple in April 1987, when it sought bankruptcy protection, sending the stock plunging again below $30. This was obviously distressing for investors who had been waiting many years for Texaco's underlying values to emerge, yet followers of McDep were able to either double up their positions or move into a stock that was the lowest ranked McDep stock among integrated companies. Then it was a matter of riding out developments in the ongoing Pennzoil-Texaco skirmish (see page 109).

4. *As you follow your favorite energy stocks, whether they are in or out of your portfolio, track their price movements so that you learn to recognize potential "support areas" on the downside.*

Knowing that a stock tends to have a floor at a certain price—perhaps its fifty-two-week low—will help give you confidence to buy a declining stock near that theoretical support level. Obviously, a support price doesn't always hold, but certain quality stocks will fall into a predictable pattern.

In 1985 and 1986, for example, Chevron continually found strong buying support around $34 a share and would rebound to around $40. But then in August 1986, as it slumped again toward $34, it touched $34½ and never looked back, eventually peaking at $64. The moral here is that you shouldn't play the technical game too rigorously. One of my clients was determined to buy Chevron "under $34," but he never got aboard; trying to save a half point or so, he subsequently missed a potential 30-point runup in this undervalued blue-chip company.

5. *The seasonal influences on oil and gas stocks can't be ignored, given their logical effect on many investors, but you shouldn't overemphasize these factors in your "buy" decisions.*

Characteristically, for instance, oil and gas stocks perform well going into the winter as investors conjure up visions of bitter cold weather, but if these frigid conditions fail to materialize, energy stocks often slump. Conversely, record-setting cold snaps across the country help send investors flocking to these stocks. Yet two or three weeks later, as spring approaches, many of these same investors again overreact as they realize that April is traditionally the low point of the year for crude oil prices because the peak of winter consumption has passed, the summer driving season hasn't yet begun, and there is no urgency to build inventories for the coming winter.

So who's to say *when* you should be in there buying (or selling)? The wise investors will simply wait for these seasonal factors to create buying (and selling) opportunities, using McDep as a key selective factor. Your goal should be to invest for the long haul in undervalued companies and not to try to "trade" the market by guessing which way oil prices will move from week to week or month to month, depending on weather conditions or the ongoing disputes within OPEC.

6. *Traditionally, if you are pessimistic about the stock market's prospects, you ought to be more interested in oil and gas stocks.* Although energy stocks marched right along with the market as it roared through 2,000 and past 2,700 in 1987, that was an unusual pattern. Throughout most of my career, when I've been frowning about my stocks, most of the other analysts covering other segments of the economy were smiling, for they had the "hot" products to sell. Yet when the market runs out of steam, there's often a shift to oil and gas stocks as an alternative. That's why I remained optimistic following the crash in October 1987, which created across-the-board bargains among the stocks featured in this book.

7. *Try to retain a contrarian spirit if oil prices begin to slump and remain depressed, for this investment attitude will help you earn outsized profits over the long haul.*

When crude oil futures were flirting with $10 a barrel in June 1986, the true contrarian investors were buying oil and gas stocks when most everybody else was selling. These contrarians saw bankruptcies in the industry, listened to universal pessimism about the industry's future, and instinctively sensed that there had to be some extraordinary opportunities in most energy stocks. When New York City was near bankruptcy, that was a great time to buy New York real estate. Chrysler and the savings and loans stocks offered similar spectacular gains for contrarian investors.

From the time oil prices began to collapse, starting in early December 1985, I kept encouraging my clients to retain their energy holdings and even to do some selective buying. "You have to be prepared for volatility and you obviously don't want to be overextended," I advised one money manager, "but if you have an investment in the best companies and you can ride out the storm, you should make some good money."

As it turned out, my ongoing recommendations had a total return of 31 percent in 1986, with even stronger gains in 1987. All through this period I retained an optimistic outlook for oil and gas stocks because I knew there was considerable institutional skepticism toward the industry's prospects and that many big-money investors wanted to see even greater weakness in the energy stocks before stepping in to buy. I took comfort in that high level of pessimism because it meant to me that there was still a lot of upward potential ahead for oil and gas stocks. When there isn't any worry among investors, and especially when most all the other analysts on Wall Street agree with my outlook, then I start to worry and I become quite suspicious about the future, knowing too many stocks have become overpriced.

You should find it easier to invest with a contrarian spirit once you have established initial positions in several of my recommended stocks. As I've pointed out, when an industry is under siege, the typical investor holds back from buying stocks in this sector as they decline, or waits patiently, vowing to pay a "bargain" price for these fallen stocks. Unfortunately, most of these investors lose their nerve when these stocks actually reach a turning point (as seen in retrospect). Instead of buying, they wait to confirm a bottom, but by then the stocks they might want to buy are often many points higher, further discouraging a purchase.

Missing a stock at a bargain price is much less likely to happen if you already own half your intended position as it heads down. For one thing, you're motivated to fill out your position at a lower price so that you can lower your overall cost basis, thus making your original purchase look a bit wiser. Also, you'll tend to become a better student of stocks you actually own—following company developments and learning to interpret stock price trends—and this knowledge should provide greater confidence about adding to an existing position at lower prices.

SELLING YOUR STOCKS

After all is said and done, let's not forget what we're working toward—selling stocks at a profit. While I emphasize long-term patience as an investor, I also recognize the importance of selling some of your winners along the way and reinvesting your capital in lower-McDep companies within the energy sector.

When it comes to cashing in on your investment in a particular company, let's start with the most optimistic scenario: a takeover attempt.

Out of the twenty-eight stocks I recommended between 1976 and 1986, eleven were ultimately acquired in takeovers and two (Unocal and Phillips) were subject to tender offers. Thus the chances are good that one or more of your energy stocks will be the subject of a major corporate transaction that gives you an advantageous, but tricky, selling opportunity.

Not having the kind of information needed to make a confident decision either way, my normal strategy is to sell half a position on the takeover bid and hold the rest for the final deal. That allows you to skim off some profits on the stock's initial runup when the announcement is made, but gives you a chance to sell at an even higher price when the deal is completed or a rival bidder comes in with a better offer. By following this strategy, you can always tell yourself that you were clever. If the deal falls through and the stock falls back, at least you profited on half your position and you still own a stock that is likely to remain "in play." Meanwhile, if the stock ultimately goes for a higher price after the initial bid, your patience is rewarded. That's the optimist's philosophy. A pessimist will bemoan having sold half the position (if the stock subsequently goes higher) or having retained half a position if the deal goes sour. So it all depends on your emotional makeup as an investor.

Unless you're a risk investor at heart, sell half on the bid and play with the other half. If the takeover fails and your stock drops back near its original price (or even lower), be ready to restore your original position if you feel the stock's fundamental appeal remains unchanged and hasn't been weakened by the company's antitakeover efforts. Management may now follow through with promised restructuring action now that the storm has passed, but the company could once again become a takeover candidate.

Short of an actual takeover bid, the decisions to sell your oil and gas stocks will all be subjective, relying upon your own personal instincts and the guidelines you try to follow as an investor. Here are some of the selling "rules" that have helped me succeed as a financial analyst and investor over the years, and should help you become more objective when it comes to making sensible "sell" decisions.

1. *Since my emphasis is largely on stocks with long-term promise, be determined to ride out adverse short-term developments that can tempt you to sell.*

Remember, you've investigated the companies featured in this book, you've isolated those that appear most promising under current conditions, and you've tried to pay a reasonable price in relation to McDep. So now have the confidence to ride out your convictions for a year or two or even longer, if necessary. Like the management of a natural gas production company with long-lived reserves, you want to still own these stocks when the *real* payoff comes.

In fact, an important part of "taking action" is knowing when *not* to take action, once you've purchased a particular stock. This means, for example, avoiding any undue concern about the daily and weekly gyrations in spot crude-oil prices. This volatility is now the nature of the beast and you can't let it take your eye off the inherent underlying values in my targeted companies, especially given the future energy scenario I've been emphasizing. Instead of letting a temporary decline in crude-oil prices frighten you into selling your oil and gas stocks at inopportune times, think in terms of holding on for the long pull and even *adding* to your positions.

2. *Some of my ideas take a long time to work out, so avoid letting exasperation cause you to sell a dull-performing stock before it fulfills all or most of its promise (as indicated by its present value of equity, which I supply for each stock in the Appendix, beginning on page 195).* This danger of selling too early is often posed by low-McDep companies that happen to be lackluster performers at a time when the stock market is marching higher.

3. *When your oil and gas stocks are moving up sharply or have showed a strong gain over several months, the temptation to take profits should be tempered by your use of the McDep technique.*

While the old adage "You can't go broke taking a profit" is certainly true, try to make sure there's not actually a lot of upside potential left in your winning stocks before selling for a reasonable profit.

For example, if you bought a low-McDep stock that is now approaching a McDep of 1.0 or has moved into the higher ranks in its group—and there are no obvious indications that management is about to launch a restructuring program—then there's usually little near-term upside potential and you may want to sell or at least scale back your position. If so, try to redeploy these funds in a low-McDep company so that you leave your McDep fund fully invested (providing you're still optimistic about energy stocks in general). We never know when events in the Middle East will trigger a new explosive move by oil and gas stocks.

When using McDep as a tool here, don't simply rely on my $8/$1.10 tables in the appendix. These values in the ground could be higher today than in August 1987, thus affecting your relative comparisons. Instead, use my $12/$1.50 tables in order to compare the company you own with others in its group. Also judge your company's stock price against its projected present value of equity in these tables. That will give you a good indication of just how much appreciation potential could still lie ahead.

For example, in June 1987 if I had owned British Petroleum at $75 a share—up from $43 at the beginning of the year—I certainly would have been looking to take my profits. Based on my target prices for oil and gas several years down the road, BP already had a McDep ratio of .94 and present value of equity was $83. In my eyes, staying in the stock at those levels didn't make much sense, given its limited upside potential and the greater likelihood of a major correction in that particular stock.

On the other hand, I did own Amoco, which had enjoyed a good year—rising from $67 to $88 (a 30 percent gain)—but still only had a projected .64 McDep and a future breakup value of $162. I wasn't about to sell a stock like that.

4. *If your stock has moved to the upper end of the McDep range for its group and then suddenly breaks out, be ready to sell once it appears to be stalled at this higher plateau. Nail down your profits and*

reinvest them in a lower McDep company that should have more appreciation potential.

However, you shouldn't necessarily sell a stock if its McDep ratio has moved to a fully valued level *and* there are indications that an active investor has been accumulating stock with the intent of staging a takeover or that management is about to launch a restructuring. Sensing these possible actions, try to maintain at least half a position in the stock so that you don't miss the potential big hit. I know that many investors gave up too early on stocks like Marathon, Getty, and Gulf. A classic example was Gulf's president, who supposedly knew his company's worth quite well. After Boone Pickens tendered for 20 percent of the company, the president sold all of his stock for under $50, convinced that Gulf was fairly valued. Several weeks later it was acquired by Chevron for $80 a share.

BE AN ACTIVE INVESTOR

Although my personal investment style is to buy and hold my recommended stocks, I've emphasized the importance of staying abreast of company and industry developments so that you can better sense the opportunities that arise to either add to your position in a particular stock or sell off part of that position and reinvest in a more promising stock. Instead of simply tucking your stocks away and only reviewing what is happening once a month when you receive your account statement from the brokerage house or bank, stay on top of the situation as an active investor. Here are several specific suggestions:

- Unless you plan to trade your stocks frequently, follow the old-fashioned approach by taking delivery of your stock certificates and keeping them in a safety deposit box. Your broker may not appreciate the extra work, but this will get you on the company's mailing list and you will receive all the information sent out to other stockholders at the same time. This has always been my practice and I find that I receive mailings faster than clients who rely on brokerage houses to forward these materials. I also obtain more information this way.

- Do your homework. Try to monitor your stocks at least every week, noting price fluctuations that might have an important bearing on a company's McDep ratio, especially in relation to other companies in its group. These simple calculations, using the data I supply in the Appendix, will keep you in tune with your stocks.

- In addition to the stocks you own, keep tracking the progress of other intriguing stocks in both the oil and gas industries as you continually search for low-McDep bargains. Some of the stocks you read about in this book could seem overpriced at the moment, due to developments in the past month or two, but be patient and continue to monitor their stock market performance, because several of these companies could eventually dip to an attractive buying level. Ongoing familiarity with a company you don't own can give you greater conviction to step in and buy when and if the stock comes under unexpected pressure.

In my own experience, I had long recommended El Paso Company in the 1970s. This was a pipeline company with superb gas reserves, and when Burlington Northern acquired the company in 1985, I felt they had a steal, paying far less than the company was actually worth ($24 a share as opposed to my present-value of equity of $70 a share). The acquisition gave Burlington Northern a major position in natural gas (as I pointed out in Chapter 5), though this tended to be overlooked by many investors as they focused on the company's widely recognized railroad operation.

I didn't buy any Burlington stock at first, but I started tracking the company through my statistical research, and it gave me a "buy" sign in late 1986. Burlington's stock had slumped to $54 and its McDep was .79, higher than only five companies in what was then my "first forty" group of oil and gas companies. I proceeded to buy a full position, and the stock, helped along by a roaring stock market and the recovering energy business, climbed 30 points over the next six months.

GET INVOLVED IN THE SHAREHOLDER'S REVOLUTION

In these days of greater shareholder activism and increasing influence on management, exercise your voting rights in support of important shareholder resolutions at the companies in which you own stock. Your involvement will tie in with heightened activity by major investors around the country that should help create greater potential value in many oil and gas stocks.

By focusing increasingly on management accountability and performance and less on social matters such as divestiture of South African operations, shareholder campaigns can help precipitate changes that ultimately strengthen a company's stock price—specifically, by bringing to light issues that help perpetuate or shield an entrenched management from greater accountability.

I've been an active shareholder in recent years, sponsoring ballot resolutions at the annual meetings of Amoco, Mobil, Amerada Hess, and Unocal, while encouraging my institutional clients to oppose oil company managements that have been slow to make changes that would bring out greater stock value. For example, I've twice proposed that Amerada Hess be turned into three pieces, and that Unocal and Texaco be divided into ten pieces.

In 1987, my proposal at Amoco sought to implement confidential voting in all proxy contests and corporate elections. Soviet Premier Gorbachev has complained about the shortcomings of the Communist government, suggesting among other things that there should be a secret ballot. We have secret ballots in our political elections, but we don't have them in our corporate elections; management knows how everybody votes, and that can have an inhibiting influence on institutional investors such as banks and pension funds.

Along these same lines of management entrenchment and accountability, I presented a resolution at Unocal that would have shareholders vote on standstill agreements, which are made between the management and one or more stockholders who agree not to buy more stock or to influence the management. I also sponsored a resolution at Mobil's annual meeting to rescind the company's "poison pill," an increasingly common antitakeover defense by which companies issue extra stock to thwart any hostile takeover attempt. Poison pill provisions give shareholders the right to buy additional stock or sell their shares to the target company at absurd prices. The objective is to make the company too expensive for the hostile bidder, thus "poisoning" the transaction.

Thanks to a resurgent stock market, I wasn't surprised that corporate performance was less of a hot topic in 1987. But this issue will be important again in the future, reflecting a growing shareholder awareness that low McDep ratios signal inefficiently invested resources, and those companies that are not performing will find themselves being prodded by shareholder campaigns.

So when annual meetings roll around and you receive your proxy statement, study the shareholder proposals and vote your proxy card against management when the issue seems to favor any proposed restructuring action or tries to make management more accountable to shareholder interests. If you think it makes sense to vote against management, even in a lopsided cause, by all means go ahead and do so.

Meanwhile, join the United Shareholders Association, which was launched by Boone Pickens in 1986 and publishes a bimonthly newsletter that will keep you updated on important developments as they lobby for shareholder rights. The address is 1667 K Street NW, Suite 990, Washington, D.C. 20006.

An increasingly effective shareholder revolt, coupled with more outspoken activism by major shareholders, will help make oil and gas companies more accountable and thus more efficient in the years ahead as the industry surges toward greater prosperity. This time around—unlike the late 1970s and early 1980s—when oil prices keep heading higher and cash flow is excessive, managements will be under greater pressure to reinvest those billions of dollars in wiser ways because of the existence of heightened shareholder scrutiny and expectations. I see this as a source of extra insurance to help guarantee that the stock prices of integrated oil companies, in particular, truly reflect their underlying values, instead of selling at large discounts as they did in the past.

Whether you already own a sampling of oil and gas stocks or you're still thinking about making your first investment in this sector of the economy, I trust my book has convinced you that energy stocks belong in your portfolio—now and well into the future. You've picked an industry that has weathered a dramatic drop in fortunes and is now on the rebound, brimming with enormous investment potential. I've given you valuable insights into the economic fundamentals of "black gold" and a proven strategy for capitalizing on that knowledge.

Many oil and gas stocks were already gathering steam in 1987, recovering from their multiyear lows of 1986, but as we know from history, bull market cycles in the energy business take years to run their course. There's still a long upward trend ahead of us, so get on board with some of my favorite stocks—and enjoy the ride!

APPENDIX

1. VALUATION TABLES

*T*hroughout this book I've been recommending stocks primarily on the basis of their relative McDep ratios and their ability to capitalize on rising oil and gas prices. I've stressed qualitative characteristics, trying to give you a well-focused perspective on the stocks I like, but now I want to reinforce these convictions by providing my backup valuation tables.

Much of the data in these tables are eventually reflected in a company's McDep ratio, crunched down from several dozen sources, and should lend confidence to McDep analysis. These data can also enhance your perspective on the stocks you are evaluating and comparing. If you learn to use these tables (updating McDep ratios as necessary by plugging in recent stock prices), you should gain greater assurance about the stocks I've recommended through greater familiarity with their statistical strengths and asset values.

The one hundred companies (including trusts and partnerships) that I cover with my McDep technique are the largest publicly traded companies, with U.S. oil and gas reserves representing more than 10 percent of the value of each company. Thus, a number of oil service and offshore drilling companies do not appear in my tables.

TABLES 1A THROUGH 5A: MCDEP RATIOS AT $12/BBL AND $1.50/MCF

This first set of tables for all the stocks in my McDep coverage looks ahead to when the going rate for oil and gas in the ground may again reach $12/bbl and $1.50/mcf, as occurred at the last cyclical peak in 1980–81.

I've applied these future values to a company's current oil and gas reserves as I calculated the last five columns: property value, debt-to-property ratio, McDep ratio, present value of equity, and stock price to present value of equity ratio (using stock prices as of October 19, 1987). Then I've ranked each group of stocks by their future McDep ratios. This helps spotlight the most undervalued stocks today in relation to where I think we're headed, keeping in mind that lower McDep companies theoretically have the most appreciation potential as the valuation gap closes toward McDeps of 1.0

To help you make use of these tables, let's go through the various steps, column by column.

COLUMN ONE: Price per share or unit.

COLUMN TWO: Shares or units outstanding (in millions).

COLUMN THREE: Market capitalization (in millions), obtained by multiplying price per share or unit times shares or units outstanding.

COLUMN FOUR: Debt (in millions); includes normal long-term debt, whether it is held by banks or is publicly traded. If applicable, I add recognition of deferred taxes and liquidation tax and I adjust for convertible and preferred stock. I obtain most of this information from the company's annual report. I add current liabilities and subtract current assets.

COLUMN FIVE: Market cap and debt (in millions), which comprises the numerator for the McDep ratio.

COLUMN SIX: My estimated property value (in millions) represents the denominator for McDep. This is a more subjective element in my calculations because it reflects what companies supposedly would pay for the various pieces (e.g., oil and gas reserves, chemical plants, refineries, marketing operations) if they were to buy these properties directly as opposed to buying them in the stock market. This denominator of McDep involves the same type of long-term analysis that corporations apply to their capital expenditure decisions. Using the discounted cash-flow technique, I project the cash flow from a company's different businesses many years into the future and discount that back to the present. This method thus measures the present value of all long-term property.

COLUMN SEVEN: This is the debt-to-property ratio, which I obtain by dividing the company's debt by property value. Depending upon where oil prices appear to be heading, this ratio helps investors measure risk and leverage. The higher the ratio, the greater the company's financial leverage in a rising market—much like an investor who buys stock on margin in a bull rally. Conversely, relatively low debt-to-property ratios cushion against adverse developments and provide financial capacity for opportunistic action such as acquisitions.

COLUMN EIGHT: The McDep ratio is the sum of stock market capitalization and debt divided by property. Since debt is added to both the numerator and denominator, McDep ranks oil and gas companies on the basis of an unleveraged ratio. This allows me to accurately compare high-debt companies and low-debt companies in the same tables.

COLUMN NINE: Present value of equity (per share or unit) reflects the present value of the entire assets of the company less debt, or theoretically the liquidation or breakup price of the stock. I don't calculate these values with the idea that a company should be liquidated, yet what contribution does the management of the company make if investors and lenders don't think the company is worth more than its individual pieces?

COLUMN TEN: A company's stock appreciation potential (in percentage terms) is based on the assumption that its current stock price will eventually equal its present value of equity under $12/$1.50 conditions.

TABLE 1A U.S. OIL AND GAS TRUSTS AND PARTNERSHIPS
MCDEP: (STOCK MARKET CAPITALIZATION AND DEBT)/PROPERTY
U.S. OIL AND GAS IN THE GROUND AT $12/BBL AND $1.50/MCF
RANKED BY MCDEP

	PRICE 10/19 1987 ($/SH)	UNITS (MM)	MARKET CAP ($MM)	DEBT ($MM)	MARKET CAP & DEBT ($MM)	PROP ($MM)	DEBT/ PROP	MCDEP RATIO	PV EQUITY ($/SH)	STOCK APPRECIATION POTENTIAL (%)
Royalty Trusts										
LL&E Royalty Trust	8.4	19	160	0	160	110	.00	1.45	5.8	
Mesa Offshore Trust	1.4	72	99	0	99	90	.00	1.10	1.25	
Freeport-McMoRan O&G RT	5.4	15	81	20	101	100	.20	1.01	5.3	30
Sabine Royalty Trust	12.1	14.6	180	0	180	230	.00	.78	16	31
Mesa Royalty Trust	40	1.9	76	0	76	100	.00	.76	53	38
San Juan Basin Royalty Trust	8.6	47	410	0	410	560	.00	.73	11.9	43
Permian Basin Royalty Trust	6.3	47	290	0	290	420	.00	.69	8.9	
Composite			1,300	20	1,320	1,610	.01	.82		22
Master Limited Partnerships										
Diamond Shamrock Offshore	17	51	840	0	840	750	.00	1.12	14.7	34
Santa Fe Energy Partners	18	29	520	60	580	760	.08	.76	24	41
Union Exploration Partners	17	240	4,100	100	4,200	5,800	.02	.72	24	56
OKC, Limited	4.5	20	90	10	100	150	.07	.67	7.0	115
Apache Petroleum	5.6	48	270	320	590	900	.36	.66	12.1	68
Mesa Limited Partnership	13	174	2,200	300	2,500	4,000	.08	.63	21	75
NRM Energy	2.0	114	230	40	270	440	.09	.61	3.5	86
Energy Development Partners	7.9	13	102	20	122	210	.10	.58	14.6	98
Sun Energy Partners	16	300	4,700	1,200	5,900	10,500	.11	.56	31	89
Enserch Exp. Partners	11.3	94	1,060	120	1,180	2,120	.06	.56	21	430
Damson Energy	1.0	34	30	140	170	320	.44	.53	5.3	97
Snyder Oil Partners	8.3	16	130	0	130	260	.00	.50	16.3	169
Transco Exp. Partners	7.1	72	510	340	850	1,720	.20	.49	19	191
Dorchester Hugoton, Limited	14	5.4	76	1	77	221	.00	.35	41	
Composite			14,900	2,700	17,500	28,200	.10	.62		71

TABLE 2A U.S. OIL AND GAS PRODUCTION COMPANIES
MCDEP: (STOCK MARKET CAPITALIZATION AND DEBT)/PROPERTY
U.S. OIL AND GAS IN THE GROUND AT $12/BBL AND $1.50/MCF
RANKED BY MCDEP

	PRICE 10/19 1987 ($/SH)	SHARES (MM)	MARKET CAP ($MM)	DEBT ($MM)	MARKET CAP & DEBT ($MM)	PROP ($MM)	DEBT/ PROP	MCDEP RATIO	PV EQUITY ($/SH)	STOCK APPRECIATION POTENTIAL (%)
Small										
Forest (low vote rights)	13.0	7	90	340	430	560	.61	.77	32	150
Global Natural Resources	5.4	23	125	10	135	200	.05	.68	8.2	52
Wainoco	6.3	12	77	100	177	270	.37	.66	13.8	121
Adobe Resources	7.6	29	220	230	450	690	.33	.65	16	108
Ensource	8.4	6	50	75	125	200	.38	.63	22	170
Berry	25	10.5	260	0	260	420	.00	.62	40	60
Conquest Exploration	2.9	39	112	60	172	300	.20	.57	6.2	114
Wiser	15	9	139	20	159	320	.06	.50	33	116
Consolidated Oil and Gas	1.8	13	23	80	103	240	.33	.43	12.3	600
Composite			1,100	920	2,010	3,200	.29	.63		109
Large										
Union Texas	13	85	1,100	1,500	2,600	3,000	.50	.87	18	40
Pogo	4.8	18	90	570	660	850	.67	.78	16	230
Noble Affiliates	12	44	530	400	930	1,200	.33	.78	18	52
Louisiana Land	33	31	1,000	900	1,900	2,700	.33	.70	58	75
Anadarko	23	52	1,200	900	2,100	3,000	.30	.70	40	79
Maxus Energy	8.6	113	1,000	1,500	2,500	4,100	.37	.61	23	167
Apache	8.6	28	240	140	380	640	.22	.59	18	110
Sabine	11	15	170	50	220	400	.13	.55	23	112
Plains Petroleum	22	9	200	80	280	550	.15	.51	52	135
Composite			5,500	6,000	11,600	16,400	.37	.71		89

TABLE 3A U.S. NATURAL GAS PIPELINES
MCDEP: (STOCK MARKET CAPITALIZATION AND DEBT)/PROPERTY
U.S. OIL AND GAS IN THE GROUND AT $12/BBL AND $1.50/MCF
RANKED BY MCDEP

	PRICE 10/19 1987 ($/SH)	SHARES (MM)	MARKET CAP ($MM)	DEBT ($MM)	MARKET CAP & DEBT ($MM)	PROP ($MM)	DEBT/ PROP	MCDEP RATIO	PV EQUITY ($/SH)	STOCK APPRECIATION POTENTIAL (%)
Small										
National Fuel Gas	19	24	440	400	840	900	.44	.93	21	13
Diversified Energies	25	16	390	250	640	710	.35	.90	29	17
MDU Resources	19	18	340	400	740	900	.44	.82	28	48
Oneok	25	13.8	350	350	700	900	.39	.78	40	59
Southern Union	10.3	10.1	100	200	300	390	.51	.77	19	84
Cabot	33	28	920	300	1,220	1,700	.18	.72	50	52
Questar	31	17	520	400	920	1,300	.31	.71	53	74
Southwestern Energy	20	8.3	170	150	320	470	.32	.68	39	89
Equitable Resources	31	21	650	350	1,000	1,550	.23	.65	57	84
Composite			3,900	2,800	6,700	8,800	.32	.76		54
Large										
Columbia Gas	37	43	1,600	2,500	4,100	5,050	.50	.81	59	60
Transco	29	26	800	2,600	3,400	4,200	.62	.81	62	110
Consolidated Natural Gas	30	83	2,500	1,100	3,600	4,500	.24	.80	41	38
Arkla	18	58	1,030	1,100	2,130	3,500	.31	.61	26	48
Enron	32	53	1,700	5,000	6,700	8,600	.58	.78	68	116
Coastal	24	46	1,100	4,500	5,600	7,200	.63	.78	59	145
Enserch	15	57	800	1,400	2,200	3,050	.46	.72	29	96
Sonat	23	40	910	800	1,710	2,500	.32	.68	43	88
Composite			10,400	19,000	29,400	38,600	.49	.76		87

TABLE 4A U.S. OIL AND GAS DIVERSIFIED COMPANIES
MCDEP: (STOCK MARKET CAPITALIZATION AND DEBT)/PROPERTY
U.S. OIL AND GAS IN THE GROUND AT $12/BBL AND $1.50/MCF
RANKED BY MCDEP

	PRICE 10/19 1987 ($/SH)	SHARES (MM)	MARKET CAP ($MM)	DEBT ($MM)	MARKET CAP & DEBT ($MM)	PROP ($MM)	DEBT/ PROP	MCDEP RATIO	PV EQUITY ($/SH)	STOCK APPRECIATION POTENTIAL (%)
Small										
Homestake Mining	44	48	2,110	0	2,110	1,600	.00	1.32	33	
Sunshine Mining	5.8	76	400	150	550	550	.27	1.00	5	
Zapata	3.5	21	74	600	674	700	.86	.96	5	36
First Mississippi	12.1	20	243	70	310	330	.21	.94	13	7
Reading & Bates	3.1	28	90	500	590	700	.71	.84	7	129
Moore McCormack Resources	20	12.5	240	190	430	550	.35	.78	29	48
Southdown	39	6.6	250	260	510	660	.39	.77	61	57
Kaneb Energy Services	2.0	30	60	230	290	380	.61	.76	5	150
DeKalb	22	12.0	260	10	270	410	.02	.66	33	54
Helmerich & Payne	21	25	500	0	500	780	.00	.64	31	48
Composite			4,200	2,000	6,200	6,700	.30	.93		12
Large										
Freeport-McMoRan	23	67	1,600	1,400	3,000	3,200	.44	.94	27	16
Mitchell Energy	11	47	500	1,100	1,600	2,000	.55	.80	19	78
Tenneco	43	150	6,500	10,000	16,500	21,000	.48	.79	73	70
Ocean Drilling	20	51	1,000	200	1,200	1,600	.13	.75	27	36
Union Pacific	51	114	5,800	5,000	10,800	14,500	.34	.74	83	65
Dupont	81	240	19,300	4,000	23,300	34,000	.12	.69	125	55
Burlington Northern	57	76	4,300	5,000	9,300	13,700	.36	.68	114	101
Occidental	24	210	5,000	7,000	12,000	18,000	.39	.67	52	119
Composite			44,000	34,000	78,000	108,000	.31	.72		69

TABLE 5A U.S. OIL AND GAS INTEGRATED COMPANIES
MCDEP: (STOCK MARKET CAPITALIZATION AND DEBT)/PROPERTY
U.S. OIL AND GAS IN THE GROUND AT $12/BBL AND $1.50/MCF
RANKED BY MCDEP

	PRICE 10/19 1987 ($/SH)	SHARES (MM)	MARKET CAP ($MM)	DEBT ($MM)	MARKET CAP & DEBT ($MM)	PROP ($MM)	DEBT/ PROP	MCDEP RATIO	PV EQUITY ($/SH)	STOCK APPRECI- ATION POTEN- TIAL (%)
Small										
American Petrofina	64	13.0	840	400	1,240	1,350	.30	.92	73	14
Total (North America)	15	24	360	400	760	980	.41	.78	24	61
Pennzoil	51	48	2,500	1,700	4,200	6,000	.28	.70	90	75
Crown Central (low vote rights)	16	9.0	140	70	210	310	.23	.68	27	67
Quaker State	15	26	400	50	450	690	.07	.65	25	61
Murphy	29	34	1,000	600	1,600	2,500	.24	.64	57	95
Kerr-McGee	36	48	1,700	1,200	2,900	4,800	.25	.60	75	110
Phillips	12	230	2,700	8,500	11,200	18,800	.45	.60	45	280
Unocal	29	116	3,300	7,400	10,700	19,200	.39	.56	102	250
Amerada Hess	23	89	2,100	1,800	3,900	7,300	.25	.53	62	170
Sun	36	108	3,900	3,100	7,000	15,700	.20	.45	117	220
Composite			19,000	25,000	44,000	77,000	.32	.57		170
Large										
British Petroleum	60	460	27,700	20,000	47,700	58,000	.34	.82	83	37
Exxon	34	1,440	48,000	24,000	72,000	108,000	.22	.67	58	74
USX	22	270	5,800	10,000	15,800	25,000	.40	.63	56	160
Atlantic Richfield	65	180	11,700	15,000	26,700	43,000	.35	.62	156	140
Royal Dutch/Shell	95	450	43,000	19,000	62,000	100,000	.19	.62	180	90
Mobil	32	410	13,200	17,000	30,200	53,000	.32	.57	88	170
Texaco	33	270	8,800	9,000	17,800	34,000	.26	.52	93	180
Chevron	41	340	14,000	12,000	26,000	50,000	.24	.52	112	170
Amoco	60	260	15,600	11,000	26,600	53,000	.21	.50	162	170
Composite			188,000	137,000	325,000	524,000	.26	.62		106

TABLES 1B THROUGH 5B: MCDEP RATIOS AT $8/BBL AND $1.10/MCF

These tables provide a current basis for comparing value based upon the going rate for U.S. oil and gas in the ground in 1987. By plugging in today's stock prices, you can recalculate McDep ratios for a particular group and begin your search for the best "buy" candidates.

You'll notice that I've deleted the present value of equity columns from the Group A tables while substituting a percentage breakdown of property value.

The U.S. gas and oil columns measure domestic reserves as a percentage of the company's property value. I've reflected relative advantage between gas and oil reserves as best as I can in the quantitative estimates elsewhere in my McDep calculations.

The "other" properties are divided into sensitive and nonsensitive, as related to the wellhead price of oil and gas. Sensitive properties include U.S. exploration acreage, international oil and gas production, oil service, and coal mines. The nonsensitive properties include refining/marketing properties and other businesses such as natural gas pipelines, distribution utilities, nuclear properties, gold mining, chemicals, and so on. "Nonsensitive" can also mean an inverse (negative) response to oil and gas wellhead prices, as is normally the case with refining operations in relation to production.

My intention here is to isolate the amount of value represented by a company's oil and gas reserves, particularly in U.S. properties, since that is a major investment theme in this book. Ideally, I would prefer to invest in companies with the highest total percentages of property value in U.S. oil and gas, but the purest plays are not necessarily undervalued in the stock market. As we've seen, many of the best values—and also the best investments in oil production itself—are to be found among the integrated companies.

TABLE 1B U.S. OIL AND GAS TRUSTS AND PARTNERSHIPS
MCDEP: (STOCK MARKET CAPITALIZATION AND DEBT)/PROPERTY
U.S. OIL AND GAS IN THE GROUND AT $8/BBL AND $1.10/MCF
RANKED BY MCDEP

	PRICE 10/19 1987 ($/SHI)	UNITS (MM)	MARKET CAP ($MM)	DEBT ($MM)	MARKET CAP & DEBT ($MM)	PROP ($MM)	PROPERTY (%)				DEBT/ PROP	MCDEP RATIO
							U.S. GAS	U.S. OIL	OTHER SENS	NON		
Royalty Trusts												
LL&E Royalty Trust	8.4	19	160	0	160	90	44	56	0	0	.00	1.78
Freeport-McMoRan O&GRT	5.4	15	81	20	101	80	88	13	0	0	.25	1.26
Mesa Offshore Trust	1.4	72	99	0	99	80	88	13	0	0	.00	1.24
Sabine Royalty Trust	12.1	14.6	180	0	180	160	44	56	0	0	.00	1.13
Mesa Royalty Trust	40	1.9	76	0	76	70	86	14	0	0	.00	1.09
San Juan Basin Royalty Trust	8.6	47	410	0	410	400	98	3	0	0	.00	1.03
Permian Basin Royalty Trust	6.3	47	290	0	290	300	30	70	0	0	.00	.97
Composite			1,300	20	1,320	1,180	67	33			.02	1.12
Master Limited Partnerships												
Diamond Shamrock Offshore	17	51	840	0	840	600	50	17	10	23	.00	1.40
Santa Fe Energy Partners	18	29	520	60	580	500	44	40	16	0	.12	1.16
OKC, Limited	4.5	20	90	10	100	90	56	44	0	0	.11	1.11
Union Exploration Partners	17	240	4,100	100	4,200	3,900	64	31	5	0	.03	1.08
Energy Development Partners	7.9	13.0	102	20	122	130	69	31	0	0	.15	.94
Apache Petroleum	5.6	48	270	320	590	650	74	20	6	0	.49	.91
NRM Energy	2.0	114	230	40	270	300	67	33	0	0	.13	.90
Mesa Limited Partnership	13	174	2,200	300	2,500	2,800	79	18	4	0	.11	.89
Snyder Oil Partners	8.3	16	132	300	132	150	53	40	0	7	.00	.88
Dorchester Hugoton, Limited	14	5.4	76	1	77	90	100	0	0	0	.01	.86
Ensearch Exp. Partners	11	94	1,060	120	1,180	1,400	79	11	11	0	.09	.84
Sun Energy Partners	16	300	4,700	1,200	5,900	7,000	31	63	6	0	.17	.84
Damson Energy	1.00	34	34	140	174	210	38	19	0	43	.67	.83
Transco Exp. Partners	7.1	72	510	340	850	1,200	58	21	21	0	.28	71
Composite			14,900	2,700	17,500	19,100	54	38			.14	.92

TABLE 2B U.S. OIL AND GAS PRODUCTION COMPANIES
MCDEP: (STOCK MARKET CAPITALIZATION AND DEBT)/PROPERTY
U.S. OIL AND GAS IN THE GROUND AT $8/BBL AND $1.10/MCF
RANKED BY MCDEP

	PRICE 10/19 1987 ($/SH)	SHARES (MM)	MARKET CAP ($MM)	DEBT ($MM)	MARKET CAP & DEBT ($MM)	PROP ($MM)	PROPERTY (%) U.S. GAS	U.S. OIL	OTHER SENS	NON	DEBT/ PROP	MCDEP RATIO
Small												
Forest (low vote rights)	13	6.8	90	320	410	400	75	8	18	0	.80	1.03
Berry	25	10.5	260	0	260	260	2	88	0	10	.00	1.00
Global Natural Resources	5.4	23	120	0	120	130	35	15	50	10	.00	.92
Wainoco	6.3	12.3	80	90	170	190	26	11	63	0	.47	.89
Adobe Resources	7.6	29	220	200	420	480	46	33	21	0	.42	.88
Conquest Exploration	2.9	39	110	60	170	200	65	30	5	0	.30	.85
Ensource	8.4	5.6	47	55	102	130	69	23	8	0	.42	.78
Consolidated Oil and Gas	1.8	13	23	80	103	140	64	25	2	9	.57	.74
Wiser	15	9.1	140	0	140	230	39	30	23	7	.00	.61
Composite			1,090	810	1,900	2,160	47	31			.38	.88
Large												
Union Texas	12.6	85	1,100	1,400	2,500	2,200	18	9	73	0	.64	1.14
Noble Affiliates	12	44	530	350	880	900	56	33	11	0	.39	.98
Anadarko	23	52	1,200	800	2,000	2,100	86	10	5	0	.38	.95
Apache	8.6	28	240	140	380	410	76	20	5	0	.34	.93
Pogo	4.8	18	90	550	640	700	49	31	20	0	.79	.91
Louisiana Land	33	31	1,000	800	1,800	2,100	38	29	33	0	.38	.86
Maxus Energy	8.6	113	1,000	1,400	2,400	3,000	30	10	60	0	.47	.80
Sabine	11	15	170	30	200	300	50	37	13	0	.10	.67
Plains Petroleum	22	9.1	200	50	250	390	100	0	0	0	.13	.64
Composite			5,500	5,500	11,100	12,100	46	17			.45	.92

TABLE 3B U.S. NATURAL GAS PIPELINES
MCDEP: (STOCK MARKET CAPITALIZATION AND DEBT)/PROPERTY
U.S. OIL AND GAS IN THE GROUND AT $8/BBL AND $1.10/MCF
RANKED BY MCDEP

	PRICE 10/19 1987 ($/SH)	SHARES (MM)	MARKET CAP ($MM)	DEBT ($MM)	MARKET CAP & DEBT ($MM)	PROP ($MM)	PROPERTY (%) U.S. GAS	U.S. OIL	OTHER SENS	NON	DEBT/ PROP	MCDEP RATIO
Small												
National Fuel Gas	19	24	440	400	840	820	16	1	1	82	.49	1.02
Diversified Energies	25	16	390	250	640	650	22	5	2	72	.38	.98
MDU Resources	19	18	340	400	740	800	6	13	0	81	.50	.93
Southern Union	10.3	10.1	100	200	300	340	24	3	0	74	.59	.88
Oneok	25	13.8	350	350	700	820	17	4	1	78	.43	.85
Cabot	33	28	920	300	1,220	1,450	36	5	1	58	.21	.84
Southwestern Energy	20	8.3	170	150	320	400	63	3	2	33	.38	.80
Equitable Resources	31	21	650	350	1,000	1,300	52	5	1	42	.27	.77
Questar	31	17	520	400	920	1,200	6	12	2	81	.33	.77
Composite			3,900	2,800	6,700	7,800	27	6			.36	.86
Large												
Arkla	18	84	1,490	1,300	2,790	3,100	24	1	1	74	.42	.90
Consolidated Natural Gas	30	83	2,500	1,100	3,600	4,000	35	5	4	56	.28	.90
Columbia Gas	37	43	1,600	2,500	4,100	4,700	17	1	1	80	.53	.87
Transco	29	26	800	2,600	3,400	3,900	13	5	13	69	.67	.87
Enron	32	53	1,700	5,000	6,700	7,700	18	3	1	78	.65	.87
Coastal (low vote rights)	24	46	1,100	4,500	5,600	6,500	18	4	13	65	.69	.86
Enserch	15	57	800	1,400	2,200	2,800	36	5	15	44	.50	.79
Sonat	23	40	910	800	1,710	2,400	15	4	2	79	.33	.71
Composite			10,900	19,200	30,100	35,100	21	4			.55	.86

TABLE 4B U.S. OIL AND GAS DIVERSIFIED COMPANIES
MCDEP: (STOCK MARKET CAPITALIZATION AND DEBT)/PROPERTY
U.S. OIL AND GAS IN THE GROUND AT $8/BBL AND $1.10/MCF
RANKED BY MCDEP

	PRICE 10/19 1987 ($/SH)	SHARES (MM)	MARKET CAP ($MM)	DEBT ($MM)	MARKET CAP & DEBT ($MM)	PROP ($MM)	PROPERTY (%)				DEBT/ PROP	MCDEP RATIO
							U.S. GAS	U.S. OIL	OTHER SENS	OTHER NON		
Small												
Homestake Mining	44	48	2,100	0	2,100	1,500	7	3	1	89	.00	1.40
Sunshine Mining	5.8	76	440	150	590	450	24	16	4	56	.33	1.31
Reading & Bates	3.1	28	90	500	590	540	17	11	72	0	.93	1.09
Kaneb Energy Services	2	30	60	230	290	280	29	11	1	60	.82	1.04
First Mississippi	12.1	20	240	70	310	300	20	7	3	70	.23	1.03
Zapata	3.5	21	70	600	670	650	15	2	73	10	.92	1.03
Moore McCormack Resources	20	12.5	240	190	430	490	14	12	0	73	.39	.88
DeKalb	22	12	260	10	270	310	16	29	10	45	.03	.87
Helmerich & Payne	21	25	530	0	530	620	39	10	0	52	.00	.85
Southdown	39	6.6	250	260	510	600	23	8	2	66	.43	.85
Composite			4,300	2,000	6,300	5,700	18	9			.35	1.11
Large												
Freeport-McMoRan	23	67	1,600	1,400	3,000	2,600	27	18	1	54	.54	1.15
Ocean Drilling	20	51	1,000	200	1,200	1,100	29	13	4	55	.18	1.09
Tenneco	43	150	6,500	10,000	16,500	18,500	19	11	3	68	.54	.89
Mitchell Energy	11	47	500	1,100	1,600	1,900	37	8	3	53	.58	.84
Union Pacific	51	114	5,800	5,000	10,800	13,300	13	8	3	76	.38	.81
Occidental	24	210	5,000	7,000	12,000	15,000	19	11	1	69	.47	.80
Dupont	81	240	19,300	4,000	23,300	30,000	7	8	1	83	.13	.78
Burlington Northern	57	76	4,300	5,000	9,300	12,000	23	6	1	70	.42	.78
Composite			44,400	34,000	78,000	94,000	16	9			.36	.83

TABLE 5B U.S. OIL AND GAS INTEGRATED COMPANIES
MCDEP: (STOCK MARKET CAPITALIZATION AND DEBT)/PROPERTY
U.S. OIL AND GAS IN THE GROUND AT $8/BBL AND $1.10/MCF
RANKED BY MCDEP

	PRICE 10/19 1987 ($/SH)	SHARES (MM)	MARKET CAP ($MM)	DEBT ($MM)	MARKET CAP-& DEBT ($MM)	PROP ($MM)	PROPERTY (%)				DEBT/ PROP	MCDEP RATIO
							U.S. GAS	U.S. OIL	OTHER SENS	NON		
Small												
American Petrofina	64	13	840	400	1,240	1,100	21	18	4	57	.36	1.13
Total (North America)	15	24	360	400	760	830	12	13	20	55	.48	.92
Pennzoil	51	48	2,500	1,500	4,000	4,700	23	21	9	46	.32	.85
Crown Central (low vote rights)	16	9	140	60	200	240	33	17	4	46	.25	.83
Murphy	29	34	1,000	400	1,400	1,700	19	12	49	20	.24	.82
Phillips	12	230	2,700	7,500	10,200	12,900	23	22	37	18	.58	.79
Kerr-McGee	36	48	1,700	1,000	2,700	3,500	21	10	51	18	.29	.77
Unocal	29	116	3,300	6,400	9,700	13,100	30	27	24	19	.49	.74
Quaker State	15	26	400	40	440	640	11	11	2	76	.06	.69
Amerada Hess	23	89	2,100	1,500	3,600	5,300	17	25	34	24	.28	.68
Sun	36	108	3,900	2,300	6,200	10,700	21	41	19	19	.21	.58
Composite			19,000	22,000	40,000	55,000	23	26			.40	.73
Large												
British Petroleum	60	460	27,700	17,000	44,700	44,000	2	30	37	31	.39	1.02
Exxon	34	1,440	48,000	19,000	67,000	82,000	12	20	37	31	.23	.82
Atlantic Richfield	65	180	11,700	13,000	24,700	31,000	19	44	6	31	.42	.80
Royal Dutch/Shell	95	450	43,000	15,000	58,000	73,000	8	18	43	31	.21	.79
USX	22	270	5,800	9,000	14,800	19,000	18	26	13	42	.47	.78
Mobil	32	410	13,200	14,000	27,200	37,000	22	19	39	20	.38	.74
Chevron	41	340	14,000	10,000	24,000	35,000	20	34	22	24	.38	.69
Texaco	33	270	8,800	7,000	15,800	24,000	21	42	16	22	.29	.66
Amoco	60	260	15,600	8,000	23,600	38,000	26	29	20	25	.21	.62
Composite			188,000	112,000	300,000	383,000	15	26			.29	.78

TABLES 1C THROUGH 5C: PRESENT VALUE OF EQUITY
(based on oil and gas in the ground at $8/bbl and $1.10/mcf)

Despite its shortcomings, accounting provides a consistent starting point for calculating present value of equity, which is also called asset value, or breakup value. It is what a company's properties are worth if they were to be sold in small pieces to another corporation, assuming that the going rate of oil and gas in the ground was consistent with the assumptions used in making the estimate.

Here's what each column in these tables means:

COLUMN ONE: Stock symbols are useful in retrieving electronic quotes and are used as shorthand by some analysts and investors.

COLUMN TWO: This is the amount of publicly owned stock, as opposed to stock owned by directors and officers and employee pension/savings plans.

COLUMN THREE: Book equity (in millions) is the company's book value, as reported in the annual report. I make adjustments if there are convertible securities or liquidation preferences.

COLUMN FOUR: Since the present value of deferred taxes is less than the stated value of the obligation, I add about half to equity and half to debt, reflecting the in-between nature of that liability. Corporations have the use of the money that would have otherwise gone to taxes, but the taxes ultimately must be paid.

COLUMN FIVE: The 1986 tax law increased the certainty that a liquidation tax must be paid if a corporation is liquidated. While the amount may not be due for a long time (the same as deferred taxes), I make provisions by using one-sixth of the difference between present value of equity and book equity.

COLUMN SIX: By far my most important adjustment to a company's reported book value of equity is the oil and gas write-up. Here's where the company's accounting statements and my resource values are reconciled. Essentially, I take the accounting value of U.S. oil and gas reserves out of the balance sheet (where they could have misleading values) and replace it with the present value of oil and gas property. The tables in Groups D and E will explain how I calculate these property values.

COLUMN SEVEN: All of the remaining balance-sheet adjustments fall in the "other" write-up category. This covers the difference between present value and accounting value for all properties outside U.S. oil and gas reserves. I may have a comprehensive basis for carefully estimating this "other" write-up for some companies, but my estimates have to be simplistic for diversified companies operating in areas such as rail transportation, steel, and chemicals. Where "other" write-up is close to zero, I have valued all the properties outside of U.S. oil and gas reserves and acreage at book value. For new investment in a competitive industry, book value is in effect the present value of future cash flow if the management made the investment wisely. In some respects, "other" write-up may be the most important column in the table. When investors disagree with my estimate of value for a particular company, that should be one of the first points to check.

COLUMN EIGHT: A company's present value of equity, therefore, is the sum of book equity plus half deferred tax, half liquidation tax, U.S. oil and gas write-up, and "other" write-up.

COLUMN NINE: Present value of equity divided by shares outstanding gives the amount per share.

COLUMN TEN: Recent stock prices, used in my various calculations and as reference throughout the book.

COLUMN ELEVEN: This is the ratio of current stock price divided by present value of equity. The companies with the lowest ratios theoretically have the greatest stock-price appreciation potential (on a percentage basis), often because they tend to have relatively high debt-to-property ratios and thus greater financial leverage.

TABLE 1C U.S. OIL AND GAS TRUSTS AND PARTNERSHIPS
PRESENT VALUE OF EQUITY
U.S. OIL AND GAS IN THE GROUND AT $8/BBL AND $1.10/MCF
RANKED BY STOCK PRICE TO PRESENT VALUE OF EQUITY

	SYMBOL	PUBLIC OWNS (%)	BOOK EQUITY ($mm)	HALF DEFERRED TAX ($mm)	LIQUIDATE TAX @.5 ($mm)	WRITE-UP U.S. O&G ($mm)	OTHER ($mm)	PRESENT VALUE OF EQUITY ($mm)	PRESENT VALUE ($/sh)	PRICE 10/19 1987 ($/sh)	STOCK PRICE/ PV EQUITY
LL&E Royalty Trust	LRT	95	30	0	0	60	0	90	4.7	8.4	1.77
Freeport-McMoRan O&G RT	FMR	98	60	0	0	0	0	60	4.0	5.4	1.34
Mesa Offshore Trust	MOS	99	40	0	0	40	0	80	1.11	1.4	1.24
Sabine Royalty Trust	SBR	95	20	0	0	140	0	160	11	12.1	1.11
Mesa Royalty Trust	MTR	81	30	0	0	40	0	70	37	40	1.09
San Juan Basin Royalty Trust	SJT	80	110	0	0	290	0	400	8.5	8.6	1.01
Permian Basin Royalty Trust	PBT	80	10	0	0	290	0	300	6.4	6.3	.98
Composite								1,160			1.12
Diamond Shamrock Offshore	DSP	20	440	0	0	110	50	600	11.8	17	1.40
Santa Fe Energy Partners	SFP	27	300	0	0	140	0	440	15	18	1.19
OKC, Limited	OKC	84	30	0	0	50	0	80	4	4.5	1.13
Union Exploration Partners	UXP	5	1,300	0	0	2,500	0	3,800	16	17	1.07
Energy Development Partners	EDP	87	90	0	0	20	0	110	8.5	7.9	.93
Snyder Oil Partners	SOI	88	110	0	0	40	0	150	9.4	8.3	.88
Mesa Limited Partnership	MLP	96	1,600	0	0	900	0	2,500	14.4	13	.88
NRM Energy	NRM	38	270	0	0	-10	0	260	2.3	2	.88
Dorchester Hugoton, Limited	DHULZ	86	9	0	0	80	0	89	16	14	.85
Enserch Exp. Partners	EP	12	800	0	0	480	0	1,280	13.6	11	.83
Apache Petroleum	APP	95	320	0	0	10	0	330	6.9	5.6	.82
Sun Energy Partners	SLP	3	2,700	0	0	3,100	0	5,800	19	16	.81
Transco Exp. Partners	EXP	29	730	0	0	130	0	860	11.9	7	.60
Damson Energy	DEPA	82	200	0	0	-30	-100	70	2.1	1	.49
Composite								16,400			.91

TABLE 2C U.S. OIL AND GAS PRODUCTION COMPANIES
PRESENT VALUE OF EQUITY
U.S. OIL AND GAS IN THE GROUND AT $8/BBL AND $1.10/MCF
RANKED BY STOCK PRICE TO PRESENT VALUE OF EQUITY

	FY mo	SYMBOL	PUBLIC OWNS (%)	BOOK EQUITY ($mm)	HALF DEFERRED TAX ($mm)	LIQUIDATE TAX @.5 ($mm)	WRITE-UP U.S. O&G ($mm)	OTHER ($mm)	PRESENT VALUE OF EQUITY ($mm)	PRESENT VALUE OF EQUITY ($/sh)	PRICE 10/19 1987 ($/sh)	STOCK PRICE/ PV EQUITY
Forest		FOIL	71	80	30	0	−30	0	80	11.8	13	1.11
Berry		BRY	15	80	0	−20	200	0	260	25	25	1.00
Global Natural Resources		GNR	86	90	0	0	10	30	130	5.6	5.4	.96
Conquest Exploration		CQX	70	120	0	0	20	0	140	3.6	2.9	.80
Adobe Resources		ADB	33	180	0	0	90	10	280	9.7	7.6	.79
Wainoco		WOL	89	0	10	0	30	60	100	8.1	6.3	.77
Ensource		EEE	96	30	0	−10	20	35	75	13	8.4	.63
Wiser		WISE	90	90	10	−20	110	40	230	25	15	.60
Consolidated Oil and Gas	11	CGS	80	0	0	0	48	12	60	4.6	1.8	.38
Composite									1,360			.80
Union Texas		UTH	21	−100	100	−200	300	700	800	9	13	1.34
Noble Affiliates		NBL	67	220	30	−60	400	−40	550	12.5	12	.96
Anadarko		APC	87	400	200	−200	900	0	1,300	25	23	.90
Apache		APA	89	280	50	0	−60	0	270	9.6	8.6	.89
Louisiana Land		LLX	87	600	100	−100	500	200	1,300	42	33	.79
Sabine		SAB	81	190	20	−10	70	0	270	18	11	.61
Maxus Energy		MXS	98	1,400	100	0	600	−500	1,600	14	8.6	.61
Plains Petroleum		PLP	94	20	0	−50	360	10	340	37	22	.59
Pogo		PPP	94	−10	40	−30	70	80	150	8.3	4.8	.57
Composite									6,600			.83

TABLE 3C U.S. NATURAL GAS PIPELINES
PRESENT VALUE OF EQUITY
U.S. OIL AND GAS IN THE GROUND AT $8/BBL AND $1.10/MCF
RANKED ALPHABETICALLY

	FV mo	SYMBOL	PUBLIC OWNS (%)	BOOK EQUITY ($mm)	HALF DEFERRED TAX ($mm)	LIQUIDATE TAX @.5 ($mm)	WRITE-UP U.S. O&G ($mm)	WRITE-UP OTHER ($mm)	PRESENT VALUE OF EQUITY ($mm)	PRESENT VALUE ($/sh)	PRICE 10/19 1987 ($/sh)	STOCK PRICE/ PV EQUITY
National Fuel Gas	9	NFG	98	340	10	-10	40	40	420	18	19	1.06
Diversified Energies		DEI	96	260	40	-20	0	120	400	25	25	.98
MDU Resources		MDU	98	250	70	-30	140	-30	400	22	19	.84
Cabot	9	CBT	70	590	60	-100	310	290	1,150	41	33	.80
Southern Union		SUG	88	130	40	0	-30	0	140	14	10.3	.74
Oneok	8	OKE	93	340	80	-20	70	0	470	34	25	.73
Equitable Resources		EQT	99	410	70	-90	470	90	950	45	31	.69
Southwestern Energy		SWN	85	80	40	-30	110	50	250	30	20	.68
Questar		STR	99	410	80	-70	60	320	800	47	31	.65
Composite									5,000			.78
Consolidated Natural Gas		CNG	86	1,600	300	-200	600	600	2,900	35	30	.85
Arkla		ALG	99	1,200	200	-100	300	200	1,800	21	18	.83
Columbia Gas		CG	99	1,400	400	-100	400	100	2,200	51	37	.72
Enron		ENE	70	1,200	200	-300	700	900	2,700	51	32	.62
Enserch		ENS	99	700	200	-100	400	200	1,400	25	15	.60
Transco		E	88	700	300	-100	-100	500	1,300	50	29	.59
Sonat		SNT	99	980	160	-110	240	330	1,600	40	23	.57
Coastal		CGP	92	800	200	-200	500	700	2,000	43	24	.55
Composite									15,900			.69

TABLE 4C U.S. OIL AND GAS DIVERSIFIED COMPANIES
PRESENT VALUE OF EQUITY
U.S. OIL AND GAS IN THE GROUND AT $8/BBL AND $1.10/MCF
RANKED BY STOCK PRICE TO PRESENT VALUE OF EQUITY

		PUBLIC OWNS	BOOK EQUITY	HALF DEFERRED TAX	LIQUIDATE TAX @.5	WRITEUP U.S. O&G	OTHER	PRESENT VALUE OF EQUITY	PRESENT VALUE	PRICE 10/19 1987	STOCK PRICE/ PV
FY mo	SYMBOL	(%)	($mm)	($mm)	($mm)	($mm)	($mm)	($mm)	($/sh)	($/sh)	EQUITY
Reading & Bates	RB	97	60	0	0	20	-40	40	1.4	3.1	2.2
Zapata 9	ZOS	81	140	0	0	10	-100	50	2.4	3.5	1.5
Sunshine Mining	SSC	99	120	0	0	0	180	300	3.9	5.8	1.5
Homestake Mining	HM	90	550	20	-160	80	1,010	1,500	31	44	1.4
Kaneb Energy Services	KAB	87	130	0	0	20	-150	50	1.7	2	1.2
First Mississippi 6	FRM	85	140	0	-20	10	80	230	11.5	12.1	1.05
DeKalb 8	DKLBB	89	330	20	0	50	-100	300	25	22	.87
Helmerich & Payne 9	HP	85	410	20	0	200	-10	620	25	21	.85
Moore McCormack Resources	MMR	80	260	0	-10	20	30	300	24	20	.81
Southdown	SDW	70	130	40	-40	30	180	340	52	39	.75
Composite								3,700			1.16
Freeport-McMoRan	FTX	96	600	100	-100	-200	800	1,200	18	23	1.3
Ocean Drilling	ODR	41	600	0	-100	300	100	900	18	20	1.14
Tenneco	TGT	99	4,000	1,000	-800	2,000	2,300	8,500	57	43	.76
Dupont	DD	55	13,000	1,000	-2,200	2,000	12,200	26,000	108	81	.74
Union Pacific	UNP	99	3,800	800	-800	2,400	2,100	8,300	73	51	.69
Mitchell Energy 1	MND	37	600	200	0	-100	100	800	17	11	.63
Occidental	OXY	97	5,400	300	-400	1,700	1,000	8,000	38	24	.63
Burlington Northern	BNI	99	3,500	700	-600	1,700	1,700	7,000	92	57	.62
Composite								61,000			.72

TABLE 5C U.S. OIL AND GAS INTEGRATED COMPANIES
PRESENT VALUE OF EQUITY
U.S. OIL AND GAS IN THE GROUND AT $8/BBL AND $1.10/MCF
RANKED BY STOCK PRICE TO PRESENT VALUE OF EQUITY

	FY mo SYMBOL	PUBLIC OWNS (%)	BOOK EQUITY ($mm)	HALF DEFERRED TAX ($mm)	LIQUIDATE TAX @.5 ($mm)	WRITE-UP U.S. O&G ($mm)	OTHER ($mm)	PRESENT VALUE OF EQUITY ($mm)	PRESENT VALUE ($/sh)	PRICE 10/19 1987 ($/sh)	STOCK PRICE/ PV EQUITY
American Petrofina	APIA	16	650	30	-10	140	-110	700	54	64	1.20
Total (North America)	TPN	51	220	20	-40	20	210	430	18	15	.84
Pennzoil	PZL	72	1,000	300	-400	500	1,800	3,200	67	51	.80
Crown Central	CNPA	60	220	10	0	30	-80	180	20	16	.80
Murphy	MUR	65	800	100	-100	200	300	1,300	39	29	.75
Quaker State	KSF	98	390	50	-40	20	180	600	23	15	.70
Kerr-McGee	KMG	92	1,500	100	-200	600	500	2,500	52	36	.69
Amerada Hess	AHC	83	2,100	100	-300	1,600	300	3,800	43	23	.54
Phillips	P	92	1,700	800	-600	2,200	1,300	5,400	23	12	.50
Unocal	UCL	88	1,700	900	-900	4,800	200	6,700	58	29	.50
Sun	SUN	70	5,300	800	-500	3,200	-400	8,400	78	36	.46
Composite								33,000			.58
British Petroleum	BP	99	15,000	0	-2,000	8,000	6,000	27,000	59	60	1.03
Exxon	XON	99	32,000	5,000	-5,000	13,000	18,000	63,000	44	34	.77
Royal Dutch/Shell	RD	95	37,000	6,000	-4,000	6,000	13,000	58,000	129	95	.74
Atlantic Richfield	ARC	99	5,000	2,000	-2,000	11,000	2,000	18,000	100	65	.65
USX	X	95	6,000	0	-1,000	2,000	3,000	10,000	37	22	.58
Mobil	MOB	99	15,000	1,000	-1,000	7,000	1,000	23,000	56	32	.57
Chevron	CHV	99	15,000	2,000	-2,000	9,000	1,000	25,000	74	41	.56
Amoco	AN	95	11,000	2,000	-3,000	13,000	7,000	30,000	115	60	.52
Texaco	TX	99	15,000	1,000	0	5,000	-4,000	17,000	63	33	.52
Composite								271,000			.69

APPENDIX

TABLES 1D THROUGH 5D: PRESENT VALUE OF U.S. OIL AND GAS PROPERTY

In my ongoing quest to maintain a comprehensive, reliable estimate of overall property value for the one hundred companies in my McDep coverage, the single most important factor is the value of a company's oil and gas properties—and U.S. reserves in particular. After all, oil and gas reserves represent the major portion of financial value for the McDep companies, certainly the ones I want to be investing in. This is true even for giant oil companies with far-flung refining and marketing operations.

My emphasis on reserves may seem like a logical concept, yet many investors still tie stock value to earnings (which I choose to ignore in my work). Moreover, widely available services that provide comprehensive financial data on many companies usually don't try to adjust for the value of oil and gas resources. Where that adjustment is made using the standard Securities and Exchange technique, the results can be misleading and out-of-date.

Therefore, I prefer to calculate my own oil and gas reserve values. I take a company's reserves and, through a series of calculations, adjustments, and judgments (which I will detail presently), I place a value on them, independent of what is on the company balance sheet. My assumptions may not be shared by everyone, but my conclusions ultimately reflect current market conditions. For example, my estimates are objectively verified by transactions whereby companies buy and sell properties among themselves. Also, if a company is acquired at a McDep ratio of close to 1.0, that helps confirm the value I've given its properties, as well as those of similar companies.

I used benchmark values of $8/bbl and $1.10/mcf for

219

oil and gas in the ground through most of 1987. (This was up from $6/$.90 in 1986, but down from $12/$1.50 in 1980.) The $8 is related to a *sustained* oil price of $18 above the ground for 1987 and gradually escalating from there in order to justify a present value of $8, since it takes many years to produce those reserves and bring out the underlying value.

My standard values in 1987 reflected ongoing and anticipated industry conditions, but since every company will respond somewhat differently to those conditions, I have to make adjustments in my tables. Thus you'll notice, for example, that my composite going rates for oil and gas in the ground are $6/bbl and $1/mcf for integrated oil companies, taking into account necessary downward revisions.

Here's what each column in these tables means:

COLUMN ONE: My estimates start with natural gas reserves in physical units (billion cubic feet), as reported by the companies.

COLUMN TWO: Normally, additional investment will be required to convert undeveloped reserves (UD), so I consider them to be worth about half of developed reserves.

COLUMN THREE: My first rough check on the accuracy of my estimates for present value of gas reserves is the reserve-life index, or r/p ratio (measured in years). I obtain this ratio by dividing year-end reserves by production output. Then I adjust for undeveloped reserves by subtracting half the UD percentage from the r/p ratio. Although some reserve estimates are either understated or overstated by certain companies, high r/p ratios suggest quality in most cases.

COLUMN FOUR: The next most important indicator of present value is the previous year's average wellhead price per mcf (thousand cubic feet). That is the best simple indication of the mix of regulations affecting the value of future natural gas production. Given the continuing prospect of price deregulation and renegotiated contracts, lower current wellhead prices signal greater appreciation potential for that company in comparison to companies with high current wellhead prices. (Wellhead prices for oil indicate quality and locations. Heavy oil, natural gas liquids, and Alaska North Slope crude typically have lower wellhead prices.)

COLUMN FIVE: This is my estimated value for the company's natural gas reserves, based largely on an adjusted going rate for gas in the ground (as provided in column six). However, I also take into account such influencing factors as the reliability of reported reserves, the percentage of unreported reserves, production potential (as indicated by the r/p ratio), the relative price received for production the previous year, and operating costs as well as possible high administrative costs, particularly at smaller companies.

COLUMN SIX: A company's present value of reserves in the ground (per mcf) may differ from other companies in its group and from my standard going rate of $1.10/mcf, reflecting the adjustments I discussed above, in columns two, three, four, and five.

COLUMNS SEVEN THROUGH TWELVE: Oil calculations follow the same principles as the natural gas calculations. If applicable, natural gas liquids reserves are added to crude-oil reserves to give total U.S. oil reserves. Also, integrated companies that have a small percentage of undeveloped reserves (Amoco, for example, with just 4 percent) may not be counting sizable reserves that could be developed through enhanced recovery methods at higher oil prices.

COLUMN THIRTEEN: Estimates of the value of exploratory acreage, or land, are tenuous, but the total is usually not too big for a particular company, given the deterioration of these values in recent years. As an example, Amoco's capitalized costs of unproven properties in the United States were $962 million, which I rounded off to a present value of $1 billion. Amoco once had the largest exploratory position of any company in the United States and that may still be true today, even after a steady decline since 1982.

COLUMN FOURTEEN: Company accountants determine book value of U.S. oil and gas properties, including unproven properties, proven properties, and support equipment and facilities.

COLUMN FIFTEEN: Ultimately, I come up with a total value of U.S. oil and gas properties, which includes all reserves plus land. I can then build this key figure into my subsequent McDep calculations. (Subtracting Amoco's book value of $9 billion from total present value of $22 billion yields a U.S. oil and gas write-up of $13 billion, which then plugs into the tables of Group C.)

APPENDIX

TABLE 1D U.S. OIL AND GAS TRUSTS AND PARTNERSHIPS
PRESENT VALUE OF U.S. OIL AND GAS PROPERTY
U.S. OIL AND GAS IN THE GROUND AT $8/BBL AND $1.10/MCF
RANKED BY SIZE

	NATURAL GAS						OIL								
	RESERVES (bcf)	UD (%)	R/P (yrs)	PRICE ($/mcf)	PRESENT VALUE ($mm)	($/mcf)	RSRVS (mmb)	UD (%)	R/P (yrs)	PRIC ($/b)	PRSNT VAL ($mm)	VAL ($/b)	LAND PV ($mm)	BOOK VALUE ($mm)	TOTAL PRESENT VALUE ($mm)
San Juan Basin Royalty Trust	283	13	26	2.17	390	1.40	1	14	19	14	10	10	0	110	400
Permian Basin Royalty Trust	53	24	11	1.63	90	1.70	19	21	12	18	210	11	0	10	300
Sabine Royalty Trust	42	1	8	1.64	70	1.70	6	2	8	15	90	14	0	20	160
LL&E Royalty Trust	12	36	4		40	3.30	2	7	2	17	50	23	0	30	90
Mesa Offshore Trust	29	0	3	2.24	70	2.40	1	0	2		10	17	0	40	80
Freeport-McMoRan O&G RT	37	0	5		70	1.90	1	0	2		10	14	0	80	80
Mesa Royalty Trust	62	6	31	1.14	60	1.00	1	12	12	14	10	14	0	30	70
Composite	520		12		790	1.50	31		8		390	13	0	320	1,180
Sun Energy Partners	2,417	23	10	1.81	2,200	.90	659	26	9	15	4,400	7	400	3,900	7,000
Union Exploration Partners	2,534	41	16	2.34	2,500	1.00	166	31	9	14	1,200	7	200	1,400	3,900
Mesa Limited Partnership	1,997	5	18	2.16	2,200	1.10	83	2	14	14	500	6	100	1,900	2,800
Enserch Exp. Partners	1,141	22	13	1.94	1,100	1.00	20	15	8	15	150	8	150	920	1,400
Transco Exp. Partners	558	30	5	1.84	700	1.30	25	15	4	16	250	10	250	1,070	1,200
Apache Petroleum	410	10	5	1.95	480	1.20	16	6	6	13	130	8	40	640	650
Santa Fe Energy Partners	203	5	8	2.31	220	1.10	24	2	6	13	200	8	80	360	500
Diamond Shamrock Offshore	208	12	6	2.31	300	1.40	14	46	8	15	100	7	50	340	450
NRM Energy	184	10	7	2.28	200	1.10	14	15	8	16	100	7	0	310	300
Snyder Oil Partners	85	20	10	1.90	80	.90	9	30	8	14	60	7	0	100	140
Energy Development Partners	112	1	8		90	.80	6	0	4		40	7	0	110	130
Damson Energy	142	31	11	2.40	80	.60	8	4	5	15	40	5	0	150	120
Dorchester Hugoton, Limited	140	0	21	.38	90	.60			2		0		0	10	90
OKC, Limited	35	59	7	3.30	50	1.40	4	45	2	16	40	10	0	40	90
Composite	10,200		11		10,300	1.00	1,050		9		7,200	7	1,270	11,300	18,800

TABLE 2D U.S. OIL AND GAS PRODUCTION COMPANIES
PRESENT VALUE OF U.S. OIL AND GAS PROPERTY
U.S. OIL AND GAS IN THE GROUND AT $8/BBL AND $1.10/MCF
RANKED BY SIZE

	NATURAL GAS						OIL								
	RESERVES UD (bcf)	UD (%)	R/P (yrs)	PRICE ($/mcf)	PRESENT VALUE ($mm)	PRESENT VALUE ($/mcf)	RSRVS UD (mmb)	UD (%)	R/P (yrs)	PRIC ($/b)	PRSNT VAL ($mm)	VAL ($/b)	LAND PV ($mm)	BOOK VALUE ($mm)	TOTAL PRESENT VALUE ($mm)
Adobe Resources	204	14	11	2.07	220	1.10	18	21	7	14	160	9	20	310	400
Forest (low vote rights)	282	17	7	1.98	300	1.10	3	14	6	15	30	10	30	390	360
Berry	12	69	29		5	.40	39	15	12	10	230	6	5	40	240
Conquest Exploration	81	18	6	1.94	130	1.60	6	21	4	14	60	10	10	180	200
Wiser	83	10	14	2.72	90	1.10	9	0	10	15	70	8	30	80	190
Consolidated Oil and Gas	120	15	21	2.12	90	.80	5	27	9	16	35	7	3	80	128
Ensource	94	9	10	2.71	90	1.00	4	16	6	15	30	8	0	100	120
Global Natural Resources	43	14	8	2.17	45	1.00	3	5	7	15	20	8	5	60	70
Wainoco	54	50	7	2.69	50	.90	2	42	4	14	20	10	0	40	70
Composite	970		9		1,020	1.10	90		8		660	7	100	1,280	1,780
Anadarko	1,704	4	22	1.59	1,800	1.10	16	0	4	14	200	13	100	1,200	2,100
Louisiana Land	677	20	8	2.22	800	1.20	62	2	5	15	600	10	100	1,000	1,500
Maxus Energy	750	5	8	1.96	900	1.20	41	23	7	13	300	7	100	700	1,300
Noble Affiliates	360	1	6	2.22	500	1.40	29	15	8	14	300	10	100	500	900
Union Texas	290	20	4	2.36	400	1.40	25	0	4	14	200	8	50	350	650
Pogo	262	8	7	2.44	340	1.30	22	9	6	16	220	10	40	530	600
Apache	297	14	7	1.73	310	1.00	11	11	5	12	80	7	20	470	410
Plains Petroleum	346	3	22	.75	390	1.10		0			0		0	30	390
Sabine	122	4	9	2.09	150	1.20	12	21	6	16	110	9	20	210	280
Composite	4,800		10		5,600	1.20	220		6		2,000	9	530	5,000	8,100

TABLE 3D U.S. NATURAL GAS PIPELINES
PRESENT VALUE OF U.S. OIL AND GAS PROPERTY
U.S. OIL AND GAS IN THE GROUND AT $8/BBL AND $1.10/MCF
RANKED BY SIZE

| | NATURAL GAS | | | | | | OIL | | | | | | LAND | BOOK | TOTAL PRESENT |
	RESERVES (bcf)	UD (%)	R/P (yrs)	PRICE ($/mcf)	PRESENT VALUE ($mm)	VALUE ($/mcf)	RSRVS (mmb)	UD (%)	R/P (yrs)	PRIC ($/b)	PRSNT VAL ($mm)	VAL ($/b)	PV ($mm)	VALUE ($mm)	VALUE ($mm)
Equitable Resources	595	19	15	2.45	680	1.10	8	12	11	14	60	8	10	280	750
Cabot	494	5	14	2.40	520	1.10	7	4	5	24	70	10	10	290	600
Southwestern Energy	206	0	20	3.21	250	1.20	1	41	3	14	10	13	10	160	270
Questar	59	3	11	2.72	70	1.20	14	1	5	14	140	10	30	180	240
Diversified Energies	117	7	10	2.01	140	1.20	3	3	6	14	30	11	10	180	180
Oneok	124	13	11	2.15	140	1.10	4	12	6	20	30	8	10	110	180
National Fuel Gas	107	4	9	2.32	130	1.20	1	3	3	14	10	11	10	110	150
MDU Resources	135	90	150	.90	50	.40	12	0	9	15	100	8	0	10	150
Southern Union	85	34	22	2.11	80	.90	2	24	7	14	10	5	0	120	90
Composite	1,900		15		2,100	1.10	50		2		460	9	90	1,400	2,610
Consolidated Natural Gas	1,066	10	10	2.81	1,400	1.30	23	15	5	14	200	9	100	1,100	1,700
Enron	1,435	24	10	1.91	1,400	1.00	36	11	9	16	250	7	50	1,000	1,700
Coastal	1,173	12	16	2.17	1,200	1.00	29	23	6	14	250	5	50	1,000	1,500
Enserch	1,000	22	13	1.93	1,000	1.00	20	13	8	15	150	8	150	900	1,300
Columbia Gas	742	5	11	2.11	800	1.10	7	4	4	14	70	10	30	500	900
Arkla	732	19	17	1.90	750	1.00	5	35	14	16	40	7	10	500	800
Transco	402	30	5	1.84	520	1.30	18	6	4	16	180	10	100	900	800
Sonat	220	34	5	2.15	350	1.60	9	15	3	16	100	11	50	260	500
Composite	6,800		12		7,400	1.10	150		6		1,240	8	540	6,160	9,200

TABLE 4D U.S. OIL AND GAS DIVERSIFIED COMPANIES
PRESENT VALUE OF U.S. OIL AND GAS PROPERTY
U.S. OIL AND GAS IN THE GROUND AT $8/BBL AND $1.10/MCF
RANKED BY SIZE

	NATURAL GAS						OIL						LAND PV ($mm)	BOOK VALUE ($mm)	TOTAL PRESENT VALUE ($mm)
	RESERVES (bcf)	UD (%)	R/P (yrs)	PRICE ($/mcf)	PRESENT VALUE ($mm)	($/mcf)	RSRVS (mmb)	UD (%)	R/P (yrs)	PRIC ($/b)	PRSNT VAL ($mm)	VAL ($/b)			
Helmerich & Payne	246	6	20	1.73	240	1.00	8	0	7	18	60	8	0	100	300
Sunshine Mining	81	2	6	1.84	110	1.40	6	5	4	14	70	13	20	200	200
Southdown	112	8	8	2.08	140	1.30	7	30	7	15	50	7	10	170	200
Reading & Bates	106	41	14	1.84	90	.80	8	26	8	13	60	13	10	140	160
Homestake Mining	73	11	5	2.13	110	1.50	3	10	3	15	40	8	10	80	160
DeKalb	52	0	10	2.61	50	1.00	12	0	6	18	90	8	10	100	150
Moore McCormack Resources	57	36	18	2.71	70	1.20	9	23	13	15	60	7	0	110	130
Zapata	109	4	23	2.81	100	.90	2	6	8	18	10	6	0	100	110
Kaneb Energy Services	86	42	6	2.45	80	.90	5	0	6	13	30	6	0	90	110
First Mississippi	43	0	8	3.33	60	1.40	2	0	3	22	20	12	10	80	90
Composite	970	12	12		1,050	1.10	60	8	8		490	8	70	1,170	1,610
Tenneco	3,245	11	9	1.72	3,500	1.10	296	32	8	14	2,000	7	500	4,000	6,000
Dupont	1,977	5	8	1.81	2,200	1.10	317	3	7	14	2,500	8	300	3,000	5,000
Occidental	2,788	22	10	1.60	2,800	1.00	235	21	7	15	1,600	7	200	2,900	4,600
Burlington Northern	2,887	26	17	1.74	2,800	1.00	93	19	10	14	700	8	100	1,900	3,600
Union Pacific	1,500	13	13	2.20	1,700	1.10	150	21	6	12	1,100	7	400	800	3,200
Freeport-McMoRan	650	12	9	2.10	700	1.10	57	22	6	14	480	8	20	1,400	1,200
Mitchell Energy	580	18	9	2.99	700	1.20	18	13	8	14	150	8	50	1,000	900
Ocean Drilling	245	48	5	2.25	320	1.30	16	52	4	15	140	9	40	200	500
Composite	13,900	10	10		14,700	1.10	1,180	7	7		8,670	7	1,610	15,200	25,000

TABLE 5D U.S. OIL AND GAS INTEGRATED COMPANIES
PRESENT VALUE OF U.S. OIL AND GAS PROPERTY.
U.S. OIL AND GAS IN THE GROUND AT $8/BBL AND $1.10/MCF
RANKED BY SIZE

	NATURAL GAS						OIL							BOOK VALUE ($mm)	TOTAL PRESENT VALUE ($mm)
	RESERVES (bcf)	UD (%)	R/P (yrs)	PRICE ($/mcf)	PRESENT VALUE ($mm)	VALUE ($/mcf)	RSRVS (mmb)	UD (%)	R/P (yrs)	PRIC ($/b)	PRSNT VAL ($mm)	VAL ($/b)	LAND PV ($mm)		
Unocal	4,500	35	15	1.94	3,900	.90	541	20	9	13	3,600	7	300	3,000	7,800
Sun	2,377	23	10	1.81	2,200	.90	659	26	9	15	4,400	7	400	3,800	7,000
Phillips	3,232	7	11	1.64	3,000	.90	496	15	8	12	2,800	6	400	4,000	6,200
Pennzoil	883	8	7	2.16	1,100	1.20	138	41	9	15	1,000	7	200	1,800	2,300
Amerada Hess	822	10	9		900	1.10	201	10	8		1,300	6	100	700	2,300
Kerr-McGee	616	21	9	2.02	750	1.20	35	14	5	15	350	10	100	600	1,200
Murphy	223	47	4	2.25	330	1.50	25	29	5	14	200	8	70	400	600
American Petrofina	239	28	8	1.80	230	1.00	33	18	5	14	200	6	40	330	470
Total (North America)	84	1	6	2.46	100	1.20	11	5	4	14	110	10	10	200	220
Quaker State	77	53	14	2.51	70	.90	11	42	8	15	70	6	10	130	150
Crown Central	79	0	9		80	1.00	6	0	6		40	7	0	90	120
Composite	13,100		12		12,700	1.00	2,200		9		14,100	6	1,600	15,100	28,400
Exxon	10,380	11	12	2.01	10,000	1.00	2,627	20	9	11	16,000	6	2,000	15,000	28,000
Amoco	10,270	8	16	2.23	10,000	1.00	1,560	4	11	14	11,000	7	1,000	9,000	22,000
Royal Dutch/Shell	6,400	24	9	2.17	6,000	.90	2,632	38	10	13	13,000	5	1,000	14,000	20,000
Atlantic Richfield	5,923	15	12	1.94	6,000	1.00	2,728	20	10	9	13,500	5	500	9,000	20,000
Chevron	7,509	6	10	1.69	7,000	.90	1,880	12	9	14	12,000	6	1,000	11,000	20,000
Mobil	7,855	14	13	1.96	8,000	1.00	1,014	15	8	13	7,000	7	1,000	9,000	16,000
Texaco	5,132	14	7	1.86	5,000	1.00	1,654	12	7	14	10,000	6	1,000	11,000	16,000
British Petroleum	1,513	0	17	1.50	3,000	.70	2,817	29	8	8	13,000	5	1,000	7,000	15,000
USX	3,436	24	10	1.74	3,500	1.00	628	8	9	13	5,000	8	500	7,000	9,000
Composite	58,000		11		57,000	1.00	18,000		9		101,000	6	9,000	92,000	166,000

TABLES 1E THROUGH 5E: ONE-YEAR MCDEP RATIOS

In recent years, a growing number of analysts have been using a multiple of year-ahead cash flow instead of year-ahead earnings as they try to anticipate stock prices of oil companies. This emphasis on cash flow reflects frustration with the degree to which earnings accurately reflect the underlying progress of the company. Earnings are subject to creative interpretation by management, whereas cash flow is subject to less control; cash is cash and it either comes in or it doesn't. Conversely, management can decide how much it wants to report as earnings, within accepted accounting principles, and even those principles allow oil companies to use misleading techniques. For example, if a company is expanding rapidly, it can expense most of that investment and cause earnings actually to go down. Yet a company that is declining or cutting back on its activities actually can have its earnings go up. Those signals certainly misrepresent the value of the company and are contrary to what investors expect.

I put cash flow to work in two ways. First, the McDep technique itself attempts to view the present value of all future cash flow. I project cash flow all the way to the end of meaningful time—twenty or thirty years—and discount that cash flow back to the present. This is a comprehensive approach, since the company that has the strongest future cash flow is going to look attractive whether we use short-term or long-term projections. Moreover, earnings ultimately come from cash flow and dividends are paid from earnings.

My second use of cash flow involves my one-year McDep ratios, which enable me to compare companies on the basis of market cap and debt to annual cash flow before interest. Some investors are not willing to accept my estimate of property value as the discounted present value of *all* future cash flow but will trust my year-ahead cash flow estimate. In fact, I ignore future earnings projections, focusing instead on cash flow so that I can compare companies on the same basis.

To better understand how I estimate a company's year-ahead cash flow (and thus its cash flow multiple, or one-year McDep), let's take Amoco as an example, based on steps I took with Amoco in 1987, after I received their annual report:

COLUMN ONE: This figure is obtained from the tables in Group A.

COLUMN TWO: Ideally, cash flow should be calculated from the top down, starting with revenues and subtracting out-of-pocket expenses. However, the information we need is more readily available to calculate cash flow from the bottom up. The process starts with net income and adds those items that are not out-of-pocket operating expenses.

COLUMNS THREE AND FOUR: To reconstruct Amoco's 1986 cash flow, we start with net income of $747 million reported in the annual report. Then we add $2,418 million of depreciation, depletion and amortization (DD&A), and $204 million in deferred taxes. The sum of those three numbers yields Amoco's estimated cash flow or funds provided from operations of $3,369 million. That's too conservative compared with what other companies report but is consistent with Amoco's traditional accounting.

COLUMN FIVE: To account for the tax effect, I multiply Amoco's reported exploration expense (exp exp) by 80 percent, coming up with $700 million in exploration expense.

COLUMN SIX: Next we want to compare cash flow from properties before the consideration of leverage (debt). That requires adding interest expense when building cash flow from the bottom up. Taking Amoco's reported interest expense as net interest and adjusting for the tax effect yields $400 million to be included in the cash-flow calculation.

COLUMN SEVEN: No further adjustments to Amoco's cash flow appear to be necessary. Where companies have taken large write-offs, it may be necessary to make an adjustment to cash flow to reflect the nonrecurring and artificial accounting nature of such adjustments.

COLUMN EIGHT: Even in a tough year like 1986, Amoco generated cash flow defined in the McDep context of $4½ billion. Almost half of that amount was from U.S. oil and gas production.

COLUMN NINE: Cash flow should be slightly higher in 1987 at Amoco, with gains in oil and gas prices offsetting possible deterioration in refining/marketing. Companies with shorter reserve-life indexes than Amoco might experience significant declines in production volume—and thus lower cash flow totals, as indicated in my tables.

COLUMN TEN: Amoco's U.S. r/p index (a reserve life of sixteen years for natural gas and eleven years for oil) is recast on a composite basis. At the same time, the ratio of property to cash flow (column eleven) should show some direction with the reserve-life index, even if not all of the properties are in U.S. oil and gas production.

COLUMN ELEVEN: My estimate of Amoco's property value ($38 billion) amounts to only eight times cash flow, slightly above the average integrated company. The implication is that the other 50 percent of Amoco's value should have a lower multiple of cash flow than is the case for the comparable properties of other companies. Skeptics would say that Amoco's cash flow generated from production in Egypt should not be worth much. Yet 1986 cash flow from foreign operations, including Egypt, approximated just $700 million, or only 16 percent of Amoco's total—hardly enough to penalize the whole company. Accordingly, my property estimate for Amoco appears to be easily justified relative to other companies and perhaps could be increased.

COLUMN TWELVE: Finally, the one-year McDep ratio for Amoco looks low. This ratio is obtained by dividing market cap and debt by 1987 estimated cash flow before interest. Investors who focus only on stock price to cash flow after interest or stock price to cash flow as reported by Amoco may miss the overall undervaluation because Amoco is a low debt company that uses conservative accounting. Indeed, Amoco is also a cheap stock as measured by the full McDep ratio.

TABLE 1E U.S. OIL AND GAS TRUSTS AND PARTNERSHIPS
ONE YEAR MCDEP: (MARKET CAP & DEBT)/1987 CASH FLOW
RANKED BY ONE YEAR MCDEP

	MARKET CAP & DEBT ($mm)	1986 NET INC ($mm)	DD&A ($mm)	DFD TAX ($mm)	EXPL EXP ($mm)	NET INT ($mm)	OTH ($mm)	CASH FLOW ($mm)	CASH FLOW 1987E ($mm)	U.S. R/P INDEX	PROP/ CASH FLOW	ONE YEAR MCDEP
Royalty Trusts												
Mesa Royalty Trust	76						2.2	2.2	2.0	28	35	38
San Juan Basin Royalty Trust	410				2		21	23	20	26	20	21
Permian Basin Royalty Trust	290						28	28	26	11.7	11.5	11.2
Sabine Royalty Trust	180						21	21	21	8.0	7.6	8.6
LL&E Royalty Trust	160				8		30	38	30	2.9	3.0	5.3
Mesa Offshore Trust	99						23	23	20	2.9	4.0	5.0
Freeport-McMoRan O&G RT	101						27	27	25	4.6	3.2	4.0
Composite	1,320							160	140	10.7	8.4	9.4
Master Limited Partnerships												
Dorchester Hugoton, Limited	77	.8	.6			.1		1.5	2.2	21	41	35
Mesa Limited Partnership	2,500	71	130		7	36	30	270	250	17	11.2	10.0
Enserch Exp. Partners	1,180	53	58			1		110	120	12.4	11.7	9.8
Santa Fe Energy Partners	580	-125	176		16			67	60	7.0	8.3	9.7
Union Exploration Partners	4,200	176	198		63			440	450	13.7	8.7	9.3
Diamond Shamrock Offshore	840	-55	120		12			77	90	6.5	6.7	9.3
Sun Energy Partners	5,900	10	326		208	80		620	700	9.3	10.0	8.4
Damson Energy	174	-152	116			13	48	25	25	9.0	8.4	7.0
NRM Energy	270		18			6	18	24	40	7.3	7.5	6.8
Snyder Oil Partners	132	-40	13				44	22	20	9.1	7.5	6.6
OKC, Limited	100	-8					10	16	16	4.8	5.6	6.3
Apache Petroleum	590	-183	263		1	30		110	100	4.8	6.5	5.9
Transco Exp. Partners	850	-346	177			34	285	150	160	4.7	7.5	5.3
Energy Development Partners	122	11	17			2		30	27	8.0	4.8	4.5
Composite	17,500							2,000	2,100	10.0	9.1	8.3

TABLE 2E U.S. OIL AND GAS PRODUCTION COMPANIES
ONE YEAR MCDEP: (MARKET CAP & DEBT)/1987 CASH FLOW
RANKED BY ONE YEAR MCDEP

| | MARKET CAP & DEBT ($mm) | 1986 | | | | | | CASH FLOW ($mm) | CASH FLOW 1987E ($mm) | U.S. R/P INDEX | PROP/ CASH FLOW | ONE YEAR MCDEP |
		NET INC ($mm)	DD&A ($mm)	DFD TAX ($mm)	EXPL EXP @.8 ($mm)	NET INT @.8 ($mm)	OTH ($mm)					
Small												
Consolidated Oil and Gas	103	−21	5	−4		8	17	5	6	18	23	17
Berry	260	11	5		1		−3	14	18	12.4	14.4	14.4
Adobe Resources	420	−44	43	2		4	36	41	45	9.3	10.7	9.3
Conquest Exploration	170	−19	23		6	6	4	20	20	5.4	10.0	8.5
Global Natural Resources	120	3	11	1	2		−4	13	15	7.7	8.7	8.0
Wiser	140	2	10	−3	6		3	18	19	12.3	12.1	7.4
Forest	410	−4	42	−4		23	4	61	60	6.9	6.7	6.8
Wainoco	170	−20	34	2		6		22	25	6.1	7.6	6.8
Ensource	102	−3	12	−4	4	5	4	18	16	9.0	8.1	6.4
Composite	1,900							210	220	8.7	9.8	8.6
Large												
Plains Petroleum	250	4	1	1		29	2	6	10	22	39	25
Anadarko	2,000	10	73	6		95	13	120	110	20	19	18
Union Texas	2,500	−57	229	6	59	6	113	345	300	6.8	7.3	8.3
Noble Affiliates	880	−64	60	−52	24	70	40	90	120	6.8	7.5	7.3
Maxus Energy	2,400	−183	391	−51	60	36	92	330	340	7.8	8.8	7.1
Pogo	640	−58	89	−51		21	92	108	100	6.6	7.0	6.4
Louisiana Land	1,800	−21	188	−12	59	4	40	330	300	6.7	7.0	6.0
Sabine	200	−35	33	−16	12	14		38	37	7.7	8.1	5.4
Apache	380	−10	84	−12				76	80	6.6	5.1	4.8
Composite	11,100							1,440	1,400	8.7	8.6	7.9

TABLE 3E U.S. NATURAL GAS PIPELINES
ONE YEAR MCDEP: (MARKET CAP & DEBT)/1987 CASH FLOW
RANKED BY ONE YEAR MCDEP

1986

	MARKET CAP & DEBT ($mm)	NET INC ($mm)	DD&A ($mm)	DFD TAX ($mm)	EXPL EXP @.8 ($mm)	NET INT @.8 ($mm)	OTH ($mm)	CASH FLOW ($mm)	CASH FLOW 1987E ($mm)	U.S. R/P INDEX	PROP/ CASH FLOW	ONE YEAR MCDEP
Small												
Southern Union	300	-17	13	10		14	12	32	25	20	13.6	12
Equitable Resources	1,000	54	25	23		14		120	100	15	13	10
Southwestern Energy	320	15	10	11		6		42	35	19	11.4	9.1
MDU Resources	740	38	30	11		20		100	100	56	8	7.4
Diversified Energies	640	-15	110	-20		15		100	90	9.3	7.2	7.1
National Fuel Gas	840	41	39	19		30		90	130	8.6	6.3	6.5
Oneok	700	34	43	23		30	2	130	120	10.1	6.8	5.8
Cabot	1,220	60	87	6	11	33	7	130	210	12.9	6.9	5.8
Questar	920	43	59	13		20	20	200	160	7	7.5	5.8
Composite	6,700							1,000	1,000	12.4	7.8	6.7
Large												
Arkla	2,790	64	76	43		50		230	320	17	9.7	8.7
Enserch	2,200	18	142			80	20	260	280	12.3	10	7.9
Enron	6,700	-81	407	48		320	140	850	900	9.8	8.6	7.4
Consolidated Natural Gas	3,600	175	187	93	20	40		470	500	9.4	8	7.2
Coastal	5,600	72	325	73		390	120	860	900	14.3	7.2	6.2
Transco	3,400	-23	293	13		130	410	530	550	4.7	7.1	6.2
Sonat	1,710	-295	196	-93		110	70	330	310	4.6	7.7	5.5
Columbia Gas	4,100	99	260	131		140		700	750	10.4	6.3	5.5
Composite	30,100							4,200	4,500	11.3	7.8	6.7

TABLE 4E DLJ U.S. OIL AND GAS DIVERSIFIED COMPANIES
ONE YEAR MCDEP: (MARKET CAP & DEBT)/1987 CASH FLOW
RANKED BY ONE YEAR MCDEP

| | MARKET CAP & DEBT ($mm) | 1986 | | | | | | | CASH FLOW 1987E ($mm) | U.S. R/P INDEX | PROP/ CASH FLOW | ONE YEAR MCDEP |
		NET INC ($mm)	DD&A ($mm)	DFD TAX ($mm)	EXPL EXP @.8 ($mm)	NET INT @.8 ($mm)	OTH ($mm)	CASH FLOW ($mm)				
Small												
Sunshine Mining	590	−119	83			20		−0	10	5.2	45	59
Reading & Bates	590	−140	41	−35		30	40	−29	10	11.6	54	59
Zapata	670	−266	84	4		58	178	19	30	22	22	22
Homestake Mining	2,100	23	59	−27	22			108	120	4.5	12.5	18
Kaneb Energy Services	290	−184	43	−45		12	185	29	30	6.0	9.3	9.7
DeKalb	270	−53	40	−40		1	83	26	30	7.4	10.3	9.0
First Mississippi	310	−23	30	−23		2	69	38	40	6.8	7.5	7.8
Moore McCormack Resources	430	−22	37	−12		8	60	60	60	16	8.2	7.2
Helmerich & Payne	530	10	60	−8			20	60	80	17	7.8	6.6
Southdown	510	−13	92			13		84	80	7.7	7.5	6.4
Composite	6,300							440	490	10.5	11.6	12.9
Large												
Ocean Drilling	1,200	−263	191	−94	10	10	260	100	120	4.7	9.2	10.0
Freeport-McMoRan	3,000	26	119	−57	−15	53	87	200	330	7.8	7.9	9.1
Mitchell Energy	1,600	8	112	5		40	10	200	180	8.8	10.6	8.9
Tenneco	16,500	139	972	84	200	800	100	2,300	2,500	8.6	7.4	6.6
Burlington Northern	9,300	−860	596	51	40	310	1,400	1,500	1,500	16	8.0	6.2
Occidental	12,000	172	906	−4	140	700		1,900	2,000	8.9	7.5	6.0
Union Pacific	10,800	−414	520	−411	60	170	1,760	1,700	1,800	10.3	7.4	6.0
Dupont	23,300	1,538	2,119	305	400	400	600	5,400	5,500	7.5	5.5	4.2
Composite	78,000							13,300	13,900	9.1	6.8	5.6

TABLE 5E U.S. OIL AND GAS INTEGRATED COMPANIES
ONE YEAR MCDEP: (MARKET CAP & DEBT)/1987 CASH FLOW
RANKED BY ONE YEAR MCDEP

	MARKET CAP & DEBT ($mm)	1986						CASH FLOW ($mm)	CASH FLOW 1987E ($mm)	U.S. R/P INDEX	PROP/ CASH FLOW	ONE YEAR MCDEP
		NET INC ($mm)	DD&A ($mm)	DFD TAX ($mm)	EXPL EXP @.8 ($mm)	NET INT @.8 ($mm)	OTH ($mm)					
Small												
American Petrofina	1,240	-25	137	-7	10	30	-24	120	140	6.6	7.9	8.9
Pennzoil	4,000	69	280	57		110	60	580	600	8	7.8	6.7
Crown Central	200	-20	46	-21	5	10	8	28	30	8	8	6.7
Phillips	10,200	234	1,097	-222	300	500	-100	1,800	1,800	9.6	7.2	5.7
Total (North America)	760	38	61	5	17	20		140	140	5	5.9	5.4
Kerr-McGee	2,700	-292	359	-159	60	70	530	570	500	7.7	7	5.4
Amerada Hess	3,600	-219	382	-14	190	100	-80	360	700	8.4	7.6	5.1
Unocal	9,700	176	933	345	210	320	-21	2,000	2,000	12.1	6.6	4.9
Quaker State	440	50	36	4		6		100	100	11	6.4	4.4
Sun	6,200	385	603	172	200	50		1,410	1,500	9.3	7.1	4.1
Murphy	1,400	-195	246	-150	56	22	343	320	350	4.4	4.9	4
Composite	40,000							7,400	7,900	10.3	7	5.1
Large												
USX	14,800	-1,593	1,559	-511	100	600	1,700	1,860	2,100	9.4	9	7
British Petroleum	44,700	900	3,200		1,200	600	700	6,600	6,700	8.6	6.6	6.7
Atlantic Richfield	24,700	615	1,646	1,096	400	500	-400	3,900	4,100	10.6	7.6	6
Exxon	67,000	5,360	4,415	-413	1,100	500	200	11,200	11,500	10.2	7.1	5.8
Royal Dutch/Shell	58,000	3,714	4,631	273	1,200	500	300	10,600	10,000	9.7	7.3	5.8
Mobil	27,200	1,407	2,471	-73	500	500	200	5,000	5,000	10.7	7.4	5.4
Amoco	23,600	747	2,418	204	700	400		4,500	4,700	13.4	8.1	5
Chevron	24,000	715	2,787	76	700	500	100	4,900	5,000	9.4	7	4.8
Texaco	15,800	725	2,732	91	400	600	200	4,700	4,500	7	5.3	3.5
Composite	300,000							53,000	54,000	9.8	7.1	5.6

TABLES 1F THROUGH 5F: SENSITIVITY TO NATURAL GAS

I began using these tables in August 1987 to highlight the approaching investment potential in natural gas and to help investors select stocks that should be particularly sensitive to rising prices. The statistics used here contain none of my judgment, except that I have eliminated uneconomic natural gas reserves in Alaska. Stocks within groups are ranked by the simple ratio of market capitalization to proven U.S. natural gas reserves.

Basically, the resulting ratio measures the sensitivity of the stock price to a change in the value of natural gas reserves, assuming that change is directly translatable into market terms. The lower this sensitivity ratio, the greater the potential change in stock price on a percentage basis. But because the ratio doesn't reflect debt or properties outside of natural gas reserves, it is not comprehensive.

In its most simplified terms, the ratio is useful if you assume that all stocks are fairly priced in relation to the current going rate for natural gas in the ground. You should also be willing to assume that the value of all reported natural gas reserves will increase or decrease by the same amount per unit of reserves.

When used in conjunction with the McDep technique, this ratio becomes more useful. Some stocks might look good in terms of sensitivity, but their starting McDep ratios might still be too high, thus stressing caution. Conversely, a low-McDep ratio and a low ratio of market cap to natural gas reserves should quickly point you to an attractive stock.

TABLE 1F U.S. OIL AND GAS TRUSTS AND PARTNERSHIPS
SENSITIVITY TO NATURAL GAS

	PRICE 10/19 1987 ($/sh)	UNITS (mm)	MARKET CAP ($mm)	U.S. NATURAL GAS (bcf)	MARKET CAP/ NATURAL GAS
Royalty Trusts					
LL&E Royalty Trust	8.4	19	160	12	13.3
Permian Basin Royalty Trust	6.3	47	290	53	5.5
Sabine Royalty Trust	12.1	14.6	180	42	4.3
Mesa Offshore Trust	1.4	72	99	29	3.4
Freeport-McMoRan O&G RT	5.4	15	81	37	2.2
San Juan Basin Royalty Trust	8.6	47	410	283	1.4
Mesa Royalty Trust	40	1.9	76	62	1.2
Composite			1,300	520	2.5
Master Limited Partnerships					
Diamond Shamrock Offshore	17	51	840	208	4
OKC, Limited	4.5	20	90	35	2.6
Santa Fe Energy Partners	18	29	520	203	2.6
Sun Energy Partners	16	300	4,700	2,417	1.9
Union Exploration Partners	17	240	4,100	2,534	1.6
Snyder Oil Partners	8.3	16	132	85	1.6
NRM Energy	2.0	114	230	184	1.3
Mesa Limited Partnership	12.6	174	2,200	1,997	1.1
Enserch Exp. Partners	11	94	1,060	1,141	.9
Transco Exp. Partners	7	72	510	558	.9
Energy Development Partners	7.9	13.0	102	112	.9
Apache Petroleum	5.6	48	270	410	.7
Dorchester Hugoton, Limited	14	5.3	74	140	.5
Damson Energy	1.00	34	34	142	.2
Composite			14,900	10,200	1.5

TABLE 2F U.S. OIL AND GAS PRODUCTION COMPANIES
SENSITIVITY TO NATURAL GAS

	PRICE 10/19 1987 ($/sh)	UNITS (mm)	MARKET CAP ($mm)	U.S. NATURAL GAS (bcf)	MARKET CAP/ NATURAL GAS
Small					
Global Natural Resources	5.4	23	120	43	2.8
Wiser	15	9.1	140	83	1.7
Wainoco	6.3	12.3	77	54	1.4
Conquest Exploration	2.9	39	110	81	1.4
Adobe Resources	7.6	29	220	204	1.1
Ensource	8.4	5.6	47	94	.5
Forest (low vote rights)	13	6.8	88	282	.3
Consolidated Oil and Gas	1.8	13	23	120	.2
Composite			830	960	.9
Large					
Louisiana Land	33	31	1,030	677	1.5
Noble Affiliates	12	44	530	360	1.5
Sabine	11	15	170	122	1.4
Maxus Energy	8.6	113	1,000	750	1.3
Apache	8.6	28	240	297	.7
Anadarko	23	52	1,170	1,704	.8
Plains Petroleum	22	9.1	200	346	.6
Pogo	4.8	18	90	262	.3
Composite			4,400	4,500	1

TABLE 3F U.S. NATURAL GAS PIPELINES
SENSITIVITY TO NATURAL GAS

	PRICE 10/19 1987 ($/sh)	UNITS (mm)	MARKET CAP ($mm)	U.S. NATURAL GAS (bcf)	MARKET CAP/ NATURAL GAS
Small					
Questar	31	17	520	59	8.8
National Fuel Gas	19	24	440	107	4.1
Diversified Energies	25	16	390	117	3.3
Oneok	25	13.8	350	124	2.8
MDU Resources	19	18	340	135	2.5
Cabot	33	28	920	494	1.9
Southern Union	10.3	10.1	100	85	1.2
Equitable Resources	31	21	650	595	1.1
Southwestern Energy	20	8.3	170	206	.8
Composite			3,900	1,900	2.1
Large					
Sonat	23	40	910	220	4.1
Consolidated Natural Gas	30	83	2,500	1,066	2.3
Columbia Gas	37	43	1,600	742	2.2
Arkla	18	84	1,490	732	2.0
Transco	29	26	800	402	2.0
Enron	32	53	1,700	1,435	1.2
Coastal	24	46	1,100	1,173	.9
Enserch	15	57	800	1,000	.8
Composite			10,900	6,800	1.6

TABLE 4F U.S. OIL AND GAS DIVERSIFIED COMPANIES
SENSITIVITY TO NATURAL GAS

	PRICE 10/19 1987 ($/sh)	UNITS (mm)	MARKET CAP ($mm)	U.S. NATURAL GAS (bcf)	MARKET CAP/ NATURAL GAS
Small					
Homestake Mining	44	48	2,110	73	29
First Mississippi	12.1	20	243	43	5.7
Sunshine Mining	5.8	76	440	81	5.4
DeKalb	22	12	260	52	5
Moore McCormack Resources	20	12.5	240	57	4.2
Southdown	39	6.6	250	112	2.2
Helmerich & Payne	21	25	530	246	2.2
Reading & Bates	3.1	28	90	106	.8
Kaneb Energy Services	2	30	60	86	.7
Zapata	3.5	21	74	109	.7
Composite			4,300	970	4.4
Large					
Dupont	81	240	19,300	1,977	10
Ocean Drilling	20	51	1,030	245	4.2
Union Pacific	51	114	5,760	1,500	3.8
Freeport-McMoRan	23	67	1,560	650	2.4
Tenneco	43	150	6,490	3,245	2
Occidental	24	210	5,000	2,788	1.8
Burlington Northern	57	76	4,300	2,887	1.5
Mitchell Energy	11	47	510	580	.9
Composite			44,000	13,900	3.2

TABLE 5F U.S. OIL AND GAS INTEGRATED COMPANIES
SENSITIVITY TO NATURAL GAS

	PRICE 10/19 1987 ($/sh)	UNITS (mm)	MARKET CAP ($mm)	U.S. NATURAL GAS (bcf)	MARKET CAP/ NATURAL GAS
Small					
Quaker State	15	26	400	77	5.2
Murphy	29	34	1,000	223	4.5
Total (North America)	15	24	360	84	4.3
American Petrofina	64	13	840	239	3.5
Pennzoil	51	48	2,500	883	2.8
Kerr-McGee	36	48	1,700	616	2.8
Amerada Hess	23	89	2,100	822	2.6
Crown Central (low vote rights)	16	9	140	79	1.8
Sun	36	108	3,900	2,377	1.6
Phillips	12	230	2,700	3,232	.8
Unocal	29	116	3,300	4,500	.7
Composite			19,000	13,100	1.5
Large					
British Petroleum	60	460	27,700	1,513	18
Royal Dutch/Shell	95	450	43,000	6,400	6.7
Exxon	34	1,440	48,000	10,380	4.6
Atlantic Richfield	65	180	11,700	5,923	2
Chevron	41	340	14,000	7,509	1.9
Texaco	33	270	8,800	5,132	1.7
USX	22	270	5,800	3,436	1.7
Mobil	32	410	13,200	7,855	1.7
Amoco	60	260	15,600	10,270	1.5
Composite			188,000	58,000	3.2

2. POSSIBLE STOCKS TO AVOID

Earlier in the book I warned that a low-McDep ratio doesn't necessarily signal a stock worth buying, even though it may be undervalued. Various factors could be impacting on the company's stock price that would give pause to any reasonably cautious investor. But how do we learn about those factors? I suggested a number of ways to update developments at oil and gas companies (in Chapter 7), and I'll help you avoid other companies with potential pitfalls by listing them here. Why take a chance on these companies when many buying candidates with sounder fundamentals and excellent prospects are available?

CROWN CENTRAL

Although this little refiner/marketer qualifies as an integrated oil company (thanks to a relatively high percentage of natural gas reserves representing 33 percent of its property value), I've regarded it as a low-quality operation over the years. The company is relatively poorly managed, which normally would intrigue me, but management is shielded from shareholder pressure by having common stock (Class A and Class B) with different voting rights. That low level of accountability to owners has, I think, contributed to a weak historical record. Moreover, Crown Central is 51 percent owned by American Trading and Production Corp., a holding company for the Blaustein family of Baltimore. (While Crown Central does show up well in my "Sensitivity to Natural Gas" tables, its holdings are miniscule in relation to nearly all other integrated companies and have a mediocre reserve-life index of nine years.)

DEKALB

This has been a relatively high-McDep, diversified company that I prefer to downplay because it has two classes of stock (like Crown Central) to solidify control by the founding family. Management has performed rather poorly, but outsiders will have a difficult time gaining control or even pressuring for better performance. Of course, any management can change its mind and sell out, or be embarrassed enough to undertake necessary restructuring.

FOREST

This oil and gas producer has a McDep ratio near the middle of its group, but control is concentrated in the hands of those who hold stock with preferential voting rights. Just as with Crown Central, holders of stock with inferior voting rights could fetch an inferior price in an acquisition or a takeover.

However, I began hedging a little on Forest in mid-1987 as statistical factors lessened my reservations about stock ownership. First, my "Sensitivity to Natural Gas" tables highlighted Forest's potential leverage in that area, which should help the stock price go up despite the issue of low voting rights. Forest is primarily a gas producer, with more reserves than any of the nine small oil and gas producers in my McDep coverage, but they have a below-average reserve life of about seven years.

Second, while Forest's staggering debt-to-property ratio of .80 gives reason to pause, the resulting leverage (if the company doesn't go bankrupt) could help the stock more than double under my projected $12/bbl and $1.50/mcf conditions.

APACHE PETROLEUM

This limited partnership has been a stock-market laggard, reflecting investor recognition of its risky future. While Apache has a high sensitivity to natural gas prices, its meager reserve-life index of five years means that a lengthy delay in realizing higher prices could prove costly as existing reserves are depleted. Apache also has a relatively high debt-to-property ratio of .49.

TRANSCO EXPLORATION PARTNERS

Transco and Mesa Limited Partnership had identical McDep ratios (1.04) on July 31, 1987. Yet Mesa's composite reserve-life index for its oil and gas reserves was seventeen years and Transco's less than five years. The implication is that a delay in realizing better resource values (particularly natural gas) could be costly to Transco Exploration Partners but could prove hardly noticeable to Mesa. Moreover, financial woes at Transco Energy, the parent company, have resulted in a dividend (distribution) cut and the antici- pated sale of oil and gas properties.

COASTAL

This company long ago recovered from its near-fatal corporate problems involving natural-gas contract woes (see page 34), and might look attractive in the McDep rankings of pipeline companies. However, I would avoid the company based on its low voting rights for shareholders.

SUNSHINE MINING

This was an obviously *overvalued* company in mid-August 1987, when it sported a McDep ratio of 1.76. Perhaps the stock has slumped a bit since then, but any future commitment to the stock should depend on your confidence in silver prices, the company's major operation before it acquired Woods Petroleum in 1985. Even though Sunshine Mining had the highest McDep (1.19) in the diversified group at year-end 1986, the stock proceeded to double over the next six months, showing how commodity fever can still override a caution flag from McDep.

(Homestake Mining is a similar high-McDep company, but is focused on gold production, with only 12 percent of its property value in U.S. oil and gas reserves.)

INDEX

247

INDEX

Production companies, oil
(continued)
sensitivity to natural gas,
239*t.*
see also company names

Qaddafi, Colonel, 33
Qatar, 9
Quaker State, 76

Reserve-life index, 16–17,
126–128
Rockefeller, John D., 77
Royal Dutch/Shell, 61, 93,
101, 111, 143
Royalty trusts. *See* Trusts;
company names

San Juan Basin Royalty Trust
dividend yield, 156
McDep ratio, 156
recommended, 156–157
reserve-life index, 127
stock price, 156
Saudi Arabia, 9
Shale Oil, 3
Shareholder actions, 191–194
Shell. *See* Royal Dutch/Shell
Southern Union Production,
117, 120

Southland Royalty, 37, 119,
145, 156
Southwestern Energy
McDep ratio, 144
recommended, 144–145
reserve-life index, 127
stock price, 144
yield, 144
Spinoffs, 72–80
Standard of Ohio. *See*
Standard Oil
Standard Oil, 42–43, 57
Standard Oil of California.
See Chevron
Standstill agreements, 192
Stocks
advice against specific,
243–246
analysis, 14–15, 20–23
integrated companies' market performance, 82–84,
85*t.*
investment strategies,
167–194
oil and gas reserves, U.S.,
15–17, 37, 38
prices, 17, 37, 54
selling, 184–189
see also McDep technique;
company names
Strategic Petroleum Reserve,
7, 12
Sun Energy Partners, 159
Sun Oil, 37, 45, 74, 88, 101
Sunshine Mining, 246
Superior, 37